Edmund Henry Garrett

Romance and Reality of the Puritan Coast

Edmund Henry Garrett

Romance and Reality of the Puritan Coast

ISBN/EAN: 9783744694766

Printed in Europe, USA, Canada, Australia, Japan

Cover: Foto ©Thomas Meinert / pixelio.de

More available books at **www.hansebooks.com**

ROMANCE AND REALITY
OF THE PURITAN
COAST

Hester Prynne and Pearl.

Romance & Reality of the Puritan Coast

With many little picturings authentic
or fanciful by   Edmund H Garrett
Published by   Little Brown & C? Boston

M·D·CCC·XCVII

PREFACE

A man might as well go to court without a cravate as to write a book without a preface.

SIR ROGER L'ESTRANGE.

HOUGH much has been written already about the North Shore, the coast of the Puritans, and the subject is perhaps as well worn as the road that leads by its sea, it may not be superfluous to survey the scene from a fresh point of view, the saddle of a bicycle. For Nature is found along the wheel's track, as well as on the mountain path, by the stream, or in the woods; and the love of Nature is our lasting

joy.   The book is then not so much in praise
of riding, as of seeing.   Nor has it only to do
with Nature, for in it is mixed much talk of
man's doings and makings, something too of
history and romance.

" *Newly-ploughed fields* "

Yet, after all, it is really the love of Nature
that rules and abides.   How often, when the
winter days lengthen and drag, the wheelman
sighs for springtime and the road!   I know
this longing, but with me, it is not wholly

for travel's sake. The longing is mixed with memories of highways where the snow melts early, where the scents of springtime are unloosened and doubled in the bland air; perfume of red-flowered maples, balsam from the pines, and a promise of fruition in the odor of newly-ploughed fields; memories of the orchard turning all lichen-like in color, from its swelling buds, and of little brooks sparkling like sapphires and diamonds in the green lowlands.

Surely, the riding is only a part! — for what of all this does the "scorcher" see, or he of the "century"? To him, too, comes, of course, the breath of wood and orchard, the fragrance from field and garden (as the rain falls on the just and the unjust); but they come too quickly, one upon the other, for the proper savoring. Besides, his mind, too intent upon the road, has no time for contemplation, nor

for vagabond wanderings, no time for summer memories awakened by familiar sounds
and odors, memories of the hot afternoons or
quiet evenings, the drowsy song of locusts,

"Rest in a shady grove."

chirp of katydid or cricket, fresh morning
rides, and rest in a shady grove, or by the
cool sea. Most people ride too fast. The
art of strolling a-wheel should be cultivated.
The best way to do this is to take the mind

off the cyclometer and the clock, and put it on the landscape and its life.

It was in such a spirit of idling and observation that the trip described in this book was made. The pictures are for the most part those one may see from the saddle, or dismount to enjoy at leisure, travelling as much in a day as is convenient. Here is no desire to impose a point of view upon others, but only to record for them that which most impressed myself, and to give such simple directions as may help them to find, on the way, whatever herein may be of interest. Indeed, the text has been written around the pictures; and it is plain that, as Stevenson said of Thoreau, the writer has "relied greatly on the good will of the reader."

CONTENTS

LIST OF DRAWINGS

THE START

"Then care away
And wend along with me"
Coridon's Song

I CROSSED the bridge over the A b a j o n a River at Mystic, under the shade of the willows overhanging the road by the little boat-house. Though just in the saddle, and barely more than half a mile from home, I dismounted to enjoy the beauty of the familiar scene. Languidly the stream glides, brown in the shadows, and, with its lights sky-tinted, glides out from the heart of the town, past the dented, tufted meadow, and under the oaks

and maples where its bolder shore rises to
the sloping fields and orchards. A good
sketching-ground: peaceful, pastoral, in spite
of the railroad hard by.

" *Languidly the stream*
glides "

As I went on, up the hill, to Symmes'
Corner, the sun flashed a million little span-
gles on Mystic Lake, and from the farther
shore the hills rose in hazy distance, rolling
toward Arlington. It is two and a half miles

to Medford Square, over a very indifferent
road, and the ribbon-like track of the wheels

Medford Square.

showed that long stretches of sidepath between the few houses were generally used.
The goldenrod was on the wane, but purple,

white, and golden asters were in their prime,
though in some places dust-laden, and all the
way the chicory spread its cheerful blue.
"Ragged Dick," I have heard this flower
called: a poor return for the generosity with
which it lends its beauty to vacant lots, arid
freight-yards, and factory wastes.   Now it
hung by the dusty roadside, and a little
farther back I had seen it springing from a
bed of cinders, and waving in the wind and
smoke of a passing train.

Medford is a lovely old place; it has the
well kept, settled look of land long occupied.
Old houses under trees that arch the street,
picturesque churches, a fine mansion turned
into a public library, — once these are passed,
the street leads down into Medford Square,
where bygones mingle with to-day.

On the left, amongst colonial homes, is the
old Seccomb house, built in imitation of the
Royall mansion, and now used for municipal
offices.   Down Main Street to the right, only
a little way, on the corner of Royall Street,

A Real Provincial Grandee.

is the fine colonial mansion itself, built by Colonel Isaac Royall after the model of an English gentleman's house in Antigua. His son, who seems to have inherited the title of colonel along with the manse, was a distinguished patron of Harvard College, having given two thousand acres of land wherewith to found the first professorship of law. He is described as kind and benevolent, "a good master to his slaves." His timidity made him a Tory and a fugitive during the Revolution, and his estates were confiscated. Great entertainments were given here, for the colonel was grandly hospitable, as became a member of the Governor's Board of Council, and a real provincial grandee.

From the square, down Riverside Avenue about a mile, is the Governor Craddock house, built in 1634: a strong, fortified brick house with gambrel roof and overhanging second story. It is one of the most precious relics of New England antiquity, one of our few old houses retaining its original form.

But our trail lies to the left from the
square, down Forest Street, a pleasantly-

Craddock House.

shaded way which soon enters the Middlesex
Fells.   At the corner of Elm Street, our road
to Melrose, there are a drinking fountain and

" Through the shadow of a graceful leaning willow."

a pumping station. To the left rise the Fells, at the back of Winchester. Around the corner, an iron water-tower rises, in black ugliness, on a naked hill. Nothing offers a better chance for architectural effect, or might be made a more pleasing part of the landscape than these water-castles, yet almost without exception they are an offence to good taste, and veritable eyesores.

From the top of the hill is a pretty coast down to the turn in the road, and through the shadow of a graceful leaning willow. Here one turns to the left, passes the Langwood Hotel, overlooking Spot Pond, and turns down the Ravine Road.

On the left is the Virginia Wood, given to the public in 1892 by Mrs. Fanny Foster Tudor; its motto: " All who enter this Wood are Shareholders in its beauty." Great hemlocks, oaks, and pines rise in its shadows from their gnarled roots amongst the scattered rocks and covert of brake and fern.

From here there is a good coast to the fork of the road, where a turn to the left leads by a shady avenue of bewildering autumnal beauty into Wyoming Avenue, and so to Melrose.

After crossing the Boston and Maine Railway at Wyoming Station, and turning to the left, the electric car-track points the way direct to where the tracks diverge to Stoneham and Saugus, at Melrose Highlands. Here there is a little triangular oasis with a fountain murmuring under some maples, and lacking only a bench or two to make it a welcome resting-place before one proceeds to the right down Howard Street.

About a mile down its length is the ancient Howard house, with a jutting second story built by the Puritan settler in remembrance of the old English home. Toward the garden is a long lean-to, and an abandoned well with a high-reaching sweep.

The car-track still points our way through Oakland Vale, past infrequent houses, patches of flowers, or currant and gooseberry bushes in rows under drooping apple-boughs.

A pretty coast.

Over a wall, by the Newburyport turn-
pike, the smooth meadow's green was fresh-
tinted by autumn rains, and beyond it the

Howard House. Melrose.

hills of Cliftondale rose blue with the haze
of autumn and the drifting smoke of bon-
fires. At the corner is a large flat rock, and
there I rested, recalling another summer

afternoon when I had sat there in the shade
of green leaves, while the new mown hay was
carried off between the buttonwoods and wil-

" *Between the buttonwoods and
willows.*"

lows. The cries of the farmers, the barking
of their dogs, and creak of the laden wagon
blended strangely with the growing shriek
of an on-coming electric car.

On the hill, after passing through Saugus, comes the first whiff of sea air, as one looks across the marshes and the clayey brickyards, under the smoke of their burning kilns, to the blue windings of the Saugus River.

Downward to Boston Street, with glimpses of the river sparkling at the foot of shady lanes and under branching elms, one gets the first taste of the picturesqueness of the old North Shore towns.   Hardly one of the houses is set squarely with the street; a delightful individuality constrains them.   It seemed to me like a corner of old Lynn, as I remember it years ago, — the great trees, the shade, the air of thrift and neatness, and, above all, the characteristic orderliness amid the general disregard of order.

The tide was inflowing, with ample eddies and a promise of great fulness.   Below the bridge, boats swung at their moorings; and beyond harvested cornfields and brown haystacks, above the level marshes, swam in the distant haze the great hotels at the Point of Pines.

But I will leave the reader to follow his
will in Lynn, stopping to visit the Lynn
Woods with beautiful lakes, rocky hills,
far-reaching views of coast and country,
lonely swamps, Dungeon Rock, and romantic
Pirates' Glen, or else to wheel on, past the
long beautiful common, and through the busy
streets of humming labor and bustling trade,
to the ocean and the shore.

THE SHORE

Here where these sunny waters break,
And ripples this keen breeze, I shake
All burdens from the heart, all weary thoughts away.

WHITTIER.

WHEN the wind is easterly, one hears the long roar of the breakers while he is yet jolting over the pavement of Beach Street, and although there is a summer hotel at the foot of the street, a sudden and strange remoteness from city life comes with the sight of the sea. To the left, a path leads to Red Rock and Swampscott. To the right, is the long and narrow isthmus of beach and road which connects Lynn and Nahant. On one side

lies the city, its spires and chimneys rising
through a light, merciful haze, and crowned
with the smoke of labor, the shore growing

Boats on the shore, Lynn Beach.

fainter and fainter until lost in the thicken-
ing mist to the westward.   On the strand
near by some yachts were drawn up about an
old hulk, in a confusion of blocks, ropes, and

drying sails. Overhead, a few gulls wheeled lazily, calling querulously, while some hundreds of their fellows perched in white lines on the tide-left bars below.

On the other side, the sea was beating in on the wonderfully fine beach sprung like a bow between the rocks of Lynn and Little Nahant. Long rollers of the coming tide, sometimes in ranks of as many as five, pounded and thundered in the morning sunlight that fell in almost unbearable brightness on their curving crests. Half lost to the troubled sight, were outlying rocks in the haze beyond the burnished light of the reflected sun, where, all mist-interwoven, blended the sea and sky.

The Nahant road is fine, and it is a charming, breezy ride. However, the wind has such an unchecked sweep across these sands, that a struggle against it is sometimes more of a task than a pleasure. Curving gently towards Little Nahant, the road rises slightly above the shore, which is overhung by bayberry, blackberry, and wild roses, and strewn with tumbled bowlders, the advanced guard of the Nahant Cliffs.

In the harbor was a tug outgoing with its tow, and from the mystery of the westward haze came, as an echo to the roar of the surf, the distant thunder of a train hurrying from one city to another. The chirp of land-birds blended with the cry of wheeling gulls; fishermen were mending nets near the shore, and cows grazing in the marshy meadows between the harbor and the sea, all in the mingled scents of field and ocean.

Nahant

AFTER passing Nahant Beach between Little and Great Nahant, our road turns to the left, and mounts the hill between the school-house, under its flag, and the engine house with its tower. One looks back over road and cottages and the crescent-shaped, foam-fringed beach to the mainland beyond.

The second turn to the left, after passing the schoolhouse, leads down the hill to a queer and picturesque temple, crowning a rock upheaved in the side hill and backed by a disorderly thicket of poplars. Columns

of rough-hewn stone uphold a roof orna-
mented with medallions in dusky gold, of
mermen and mermaids, sea-horses and sea-

The old rock temple.

gods.   Built in 1861, it is all that is left
of the once popular resort, "The Maolis
Gardens."

At the end of the shore road, by a wood-
bine-covered rustic fence and gate, a path
leads down a few rough steps and straggles
along the cliff above rocky buttresses of purple, black, and ruddy sienna, accentuated by
spots of yellow and cool gray. Down into
its edge creep weeds and grasses gay with
wild flowers. The sea breaks below on a
confusion of many-colored rocks, lifting in
its every undulation the rockweed which
shows in the coming wave as in a tent of
crystal.

Soon the path rises, passing sometimes
over the bare, shelving, wind-swept rock,
until, at the top of a cliff, one comes to a
seat of stout plank bolted to granite posts.
It commands a fine and far-reaching view.

To the northeast is Swampscott, on its
topmost point the new High School, and
away in the distance, changing, serrated
spots of foam discover the rocky islets off
Marblehead. Eastward, under the sea's
rim, the waves dash high about Egg Rock,
named from the great quantities of gulls'

eggs found there by the early settlers. From its lantern, a red warning goes forth into the night. Near at hand, the sunken ledges now and then betray their presence, as they break the incoming swell into great bouquets of foam.

At the foot of the cliff is Spouting Horn, seen best by going down at the right to the flat ledges below. The waves, breaking on the rocks, rush into a narrowing channel, and in a second or two a puff of foam and spray shoots upward and outward, back to the sea, carrying on its breast a little rainbow.

If we may credit tradition, in these waters is the lair of the sea-serpent. We read that he was occasionally seen here in the summer of 1817 by "Hundreds of curious spectators," who declared that he was as long as the mainmast of a "seventy-four," with a "shaggy head" and "glittering eye." Rewards were offered for his capture; it is needless to say that they were offered in vain! John Josselyn, Gent., who visited the

coast in 1638, averred that his snake-ship
was seen "Quoiled up on a rock at Cape
Ann." At other times, mention is made of
his appearance off Cape Ann, but Nahant
Bay seems to have been his favorite resort.

•

There is a charming arrangement of path
and shore, to a stile at the top of a long
flight of steps, fringed with graceful willows
and descending to Stony Beach; then a turn-
stile, and between the two, the path loses its
rustic character and becomes a mere walk of
crushed stone, bordering an irreproachable
lawn with cultivated shrubs and brilliant
flowering plants. Turning the headland and
almost doubling on itself, the path changes
to a plank walk, and leads back to Nahant
Road. Here is a long hospitable bench
overhanging Bass or The Forty Steps Beach,
with a fine view of a retired and singularly
beautiful cove with East Point on its other
side, and in its middle Castle Rock. So
sheltered is it here, that only the roughest
weather can trouble the cove's calm waters.

Nahant is an Indian name meaning "the twins." Captain John Smith, in 1614, named the spot the Fullerton Isles; for before the connecting roads were built the high tides may have made seeming islands of the two peninsulas. Indeed, from a vessel's deck, mariners, wary of this rock-picketed coast, might easily have thought them sea-girt.

A suit of clothes was the price paid Saga-more Poquanum for the whole place by the settlers of Lynn, of which town it was a part until 1853. Like all the islands about Bos-ton Harbor, it is said to have been heavily wooded once; but it was early cleared, leav-ing it at once as treeless and bleak as the islands are to-day. In the first half of our century, thousands of trees were planted by public-spirited men from Boston. Willows and poplars seem to have thriven best on its wind-swept turf. The peninsula was used, after its purchase, as a common pasture; then came the Breeds, the Hoods, and the Johnsons, first lords of the soil, wresting a living from pasture and sea until the natural

Stony Beach, Nahant.

beauty of the place and its healthful summer climate brought wealthy families from Boston and Salem; and amongst them were scholarly men of genius, who found companionship and help in the presence of

"The grand majestic symphonies of ocean."

Unhappily, the houses in which these famous men lived and labored have been destroyed or very much altered. Prescott worked here at his "Ferdinand and Isabella," his "Conquest of Mexico," and his "Philip the Second." His house overlooked Swallow's Cave, and has been much changed. Motley began his "Dutch Republic" in Mrs. Hannah Hood's cottage, which stood in a corner of what is now the George Upham estate, opposite Whitney's Hotel. When torn down, it was the oldest house on Nahant. Mrs. Annie Johnson, the Nahant poet, remembers well when Longfellow boarded with her father, Jonathan Johnson. There he wrote a part of "Hiawatha." The house was on the Main Street; a few years ago it

was sold at auction, moved, and entirely re-
modelled.   Longfellow also boarded with
Mrs. Hannah Hood, and later bought the
Wetmore place, and lived there many years.
Latterly, the house was known as the Long-
fellow cottage; it was burned May 18, 1896.
Professor Agassiz had also a summer home
here.

No doubt it was partly its convenient
nearness to Boston, as well as its climate
and beauty, which led these men to choose
the place for residence.   In fact, it is the
very closeness of the Nahant cliffs to the
hived life of cities which freshens and mag-
nifies the impression produced by the ocean.
Within sound of bells in city steeples, its
surf thunders on sand or rock, and the long
rumble of heavy trains is heard in the pauses
of roaring breakers.   Nowhere on the coast
is one more impressed by the sea than here.
On the cliffs at Magnolia, over the abyss of
Rafe's Chasm and fateful Norman's Woe, or
by the lonely rocks of Folly Cove or Land's
End, we may be more alone with nature,

Pulpit Rock.

but at Nahant the sharp contrast between
the city and the shore is felt with keenest
pleasure.

At the end of Nahant Road, on the other
side of Bass Beach and Castle Rock, there is
a path passing, at the rear of Henry Cabot
Lodge's house, up rough steps by sumachs
and struggling poplars, to the cliffs; and
here is a grand view of Boston Harbor and
Massachusets Bay.

Directly underneath is Pulpit Rock, a
great mass jutting out over the water, and
named from its fancied resemblance to a pulpit. On its top is the suggestion of a Bible
and prayer-book. At its left, in the chasm
crossed by the little wooden bridge, is an
arch called the Natural Bridge, and at the
right is Sappho's Rock. The walk overhanging the hollow, resounding chasms and
jagged ledges leads on to East Point, a van-
tage ground for viewing the surf; even on
a calm day it rushes angrily over the ledges,
to be churned to foam against the resisting

rocks. A great hotel, the pride of the coast, was built here in 1824, and was burned in 1861. All that is left of it now is the billiard-hall, a little temple-like structure crowning the Point, lonely and picturesque.

Swallow's Cave.

After returning to Nahant Road, the first turn to the left leads past the oddly placed little delta of vegetable garden, shrub and flower-hid, to the shore, westward. Here is Swallow's Cave, said to be seventy feet deep,

fourteen feet wide in places, and as much as
twenty feet in height. I know nothing to
the contrary; and advise all doubters to for-
sake the wheel for a dory, and make what
should be a most interesting investigation.

Longfellow Cottage.

On the way back, the first left leads to
Cliff Street, and a pretty vine-clad church;
whence, by turning again to the left, one
comes to Willow Road, the way to Bass
Point and West Cliff, thus completing the

circuit of Great Nahant, and leading back
to Nahant Road and Lynn.

Just around the corner of Cliff Street, on
Willow Road, stood the Longfellow cottage.
It was French roofed, and had sightly ver-
andas.   A large window in the roof lighted
the studio of the poet's artist son.   At the
back, it overlooked all Boston Harbor.   Here
the poet lived and wrote in sight and hear-
ing of the sea.

> "Ah! what pleasant visions haunt me
>   As I gaze upon the sea!
> All the old romantic legends,
>   All my dreams, come back to me." [1]

Across Lynn Bar, as the harbor is called,
over the headland, when day is done, still
come the "sounds aërial" of the bells of
Lynn.   A few years ago, an order was in-
troduced in the city government to stop the
ringing of these evening bells.   But too many
of the old stock still lived, in whose hearts,
from childhood, this New England angelus
had found an echo; and so the Philistines

---

[1] The Secret of the Sea.

were routed.   As they came to the poet so
long ago, they still come —

" Borne on the evening wind across the crimson twilight."

   .   .   .   .

" The distant lighthouse hears, and with his flaming
   signal
   Answers you, passing the watchword on, O Bells of
   Lynn !

" And down the darkening coast run the tumultuous
   surges,
   And clap their hands, and shout to you, O Bells of
   Lynn !

" Till from the shuddering sea, with your wild incanta-
   tions,
   Ye summon up the spectral moon, O Bells of Lynn !

" And startled at the sight, like the weird woman of
   Endor,
   Ye cry aloud, and then are still, O Bells of Lynn ! "

Lynn and Swampscott

LITTLE is left in Lynn of old times, for it has changed wonderfully. It seems not long ago that much of the manufacturing was done in the little door-yard shops, once so common, or in the homes themselves. The spare minutes of every housewife were given to binding shoes. Piles of flat-folded vamps stood in some handy corner, and near by the women sat and day-dreamed, or gossiped as they sewed. Now all work is done in the great factories of this the greatest "shoe town" in the world.

Such a bustling city seems an unlikely home for romance. Yet under the shadow of High Rock lived Moll Pitcher, witch and

fortune-teller; in the fastnesses of Lynn
Woods pirates made their
lair, and, if we may be-
lieve tradition, Dungeon
Rock still guards
ill-gotten treasure.

When the shoe-
shops and mills of
busy Lynn, and
noise, and stone-
paved roads have
been left behind,
there comes the
evidence of pros-
perity and rewarded in-
dustry with the well-kept
roads, villa-lined, to Swampscott. It is a mile and
more of good wheeling
from the fine colonial
house of the Oxford Club,
by Nahant and Ocean Streets, to Humphrey
Street, in concentric curve with King's Beach.[1]

Moll Pitcher

[1] Lewis calls this Humphrey's Beach.

First of the Swampscott beaches, it is separated from the road by old fish-houses and modest cottages whose erratic back-yards, gay with the yellow of sunflowers and nasturtiums, make a bright background to the oddly-littered sands, — sands gray, moist, soft underfoot, fit for old-fashioned sanded floors in country inns and kitchens. Fish-nets hang drying from the garden fences, or trail their sinuous length along the beach. Lobster-pots, and fish-cars, buoys, blocks, floats, and anchors lie about the sands and the drawn up dories.

The Swampscott dory is the safest of boats, if handled properly, and any one needs a good boat who must gain his living over the sunken ledges of this perilous coast. It is a picturesque sight to see the fishermen set forth or come in through the morning surf. In former years a large fleet of vessels sailed from Swampscott for deep-sea fishing, summer and winter. Now, only a few are left, and most of the fishing is done from dories near the shore. " Fish are scurce," is the complaint; and the appearance of weirs along the coast seems to promise that they may be "scurcer." There is no harbor, and

Fisherman's Beach.

the boats lie at moorings off the beaches in Nahant Bay.

Next comes Blaney's or Fisherman's Beach, longer, busier, with more dories, fishermen,

and fish-houses, — the real fishing centre.
Before reaching it, the road, always with
glimpses of the sea, passes the soldiers'
monument, backed by very fine residences,
on streets laid out through Paradise Woods.

Orient Street follows the shore closely, and
where it turns away from the beach there is
a pleasant look backward over the bay and
town. From the shore of mingled rock and
sand, the land rises in diversified and cultivated beauty, and stretches away westward to
the shores of Lynn and Nahant. The road
is perfect, and one is tempted to covet the
shaded seats on these lawns, lulled by the
sea.

From the little summer-house overlooking
Whale Beach, opposite the Ocean House, may
be seen the cliffs of the South Shore at Scitu-
ate, showing faintly beyond Nahant and Egg
Rock. To the left, the beach curves sharply
to the wooded shore of Phillips' Point,
Tedesco Rocks, and Dread Ledge.

The ledge's ominous name might well be
borne by all the rocky chain of reefs and

rocks off this dangerous coast. While the
summer wind just fringes them with white, it
is hard to imagine how awful and sinister is
their aspect when swept by the black waters
of winter tempests. One January night, in
1857, the ship Tedesco was lost on those
cruel rocks, and all on board perished pite-
ously. The tormented sea tore and ground
the vessel piece-meal, and then hurled her
great anchors after the débris high upon the
resisting rocks; and there they were found in
the morning by the townsmen, amid the other
wreckage, and the dead bodies, all awful witnesses of the sea's mighty power.

But in cycling weather all is peace, and
from the sunny beach the road rises over the
point to the dense cool shade of giant willows
and maples. Then, as it grows sunny again,
oaks begin to mingle with the willows, which
seem to be the typical trees of Swampscott.
Under their branches the old stone walls are
fringed with sumachs and birches, and rocky
ledges crop out from their coverings of sweet

fern and bayberry. Suddenly cool breezes
come again from the sea, and, over the waving roadside tansy and goldenrod, glimpses of
blue water between swaying trees; then, seen
across green level fields, rise the picturesque
profiles of Clifton and Marblehead Neck.

From Humphrey Square, level and broad
Atlantic Avenue is lined on one side with
fine residences of the modern American type,
which at its best is often extremely picturesque, while on the other side the unoccu-
pied land slopes gently to Phillips' Pond and
Beach, and is crossed by a pretty lane under
apple-boughs drooping with reddening fruit.
In springtime their white and pink blossoms
count, in telling masses, against the tender
blues and greens of sky and water.

In fact, this " stern and rock bound coast "
is richly beautiful in color. Beyond Beach
Bluff, its craggy hillsides are dotted with
softly rounded clumps of willow, turning silver in the breeze, though touched by autumn
with lemon yellow, the slopes and marshy
places are splashed broadly with goldenrod

and tansy, with the dull rich red of Joe Pye
Weed, and the sombre purple of ripe elder-
berries; in the hollows, squares of strange
blue, green, and dye-like purple cabbages
alternate with pumpkins and squashes in
every gradation of yellow and orange; and
all this brightness is interwoven with the
bronze greens and browns of foliage made
splendid here and there by the scarlets and
gold of early autumn leaves.

Marblehead

WHEN one turns again toward the sea, it is by the little greenhouse and the bit of meadow made gay by bunches of changeful hydrangeas and flaming cannas. The large house across the fields, over the strong stone wall, is the Devereux Mansion, — a modern house on the site of the old farmhouse visited by Longfellow in 1846, and celebrated in his poem "The Fire of Driftwood."

> " We sat within the farmhouse old,
>   Whose windows, looking o'er the bay,
> Gave to the sea-breeze damp and cold
>   An easy entrance night and day."

The farmhouse has been gone a long time, and the farm itself cut up into many house-lots; but the good old-fashioned barn still opens its wide doors at the end of the lovely elm-shaded approach.

Here, through the warm summer afternoons and evenings, the air is filled with the rumble of car-

Eastern Yacht Club.

riages rolling through the narrow street; for it is a favorite drive, and leads past the ruins of the old fort and over the narrow

causeway by Marblehead Beach to Marblehead Neck.

All around this rugged peninsula are fine
drives and walks, with broad ocean views on
one side, and on the other pleasant outlooks
over the harbor to the old town.   Here are
the headquarters of yachting in the East, and
the houses of the Eastern and Corinthian
yacht clubs.

About the shore are curious formations in
the rocks, and grand places for watching the
eddying tides, either in upspringing surf or
restful open sea.   But the finest entertain-
ment Marblehead offers is not there, but
rather on the harbor side, at sunset.   Then
the old town, rising with picturesque profile,
is empurpled against the richly luminous
sky, and the calm deep waters of the harbor
reflect the glowing colors of a picture remem-
bered with delight.

The way to the old town by land is back
over the causeway and then to the right.   A
little brook comes from the pond by the

Devereux Mansion under great trees, and, after crossing the road, wanders off through the meadow beyond which lies Marblehead.

> " The strange old-fashioned silent town,
>   The lighthouse, the dismantled fort,
>   The wooden houses quaint and brown."

Was the color adjective well chosen? "Gray" would have been more truthful. I remember Marblehead years ago, much less tricked out with paint. When I was looking for the scenes of Agnes Surriage's girlhood, not long ago, Old Floyd Oirson's house was clothed with that soft gray mantle which our New England weather casts over unpainted wood. Now it is bright yellow!

This passion or necessity for paint, varying in tint with the caprice of house-owners, is the reason our towns have such a motley color-effect. In the Old Country, the building is mostly of stone, generally quarried in the neighborhood. This gives a uniform breadth of effect, and is in subtle harmony

with the landscape.   Here, on the contrary,
we may have a cinnamon-colored house between one of a virulent green and another of
a bilious blue, these in turn flanked by
pumpkin yellow and slaughter-house red.
Where the colors are not so "loud," they
simply run the scale of the dealer's sample-
card of ready-mixed tints.[1]   There is the
same difference between the natural color
of stone or wood and of paint, that there is
between the fresh complexion of a young
girl and the rouged and powdered cheeks of
an actress.

Washington, when he visited New England, in 1789, marvelled at the houses "being
built almost entirely of wood . . . as the
country is full of stone, and good clay for
bricks."   The people told him that "on
account of the fog and the damp they deemed
them wholesomer, and for that reason pre-

[1] Ruskin says somewhere (I think in " Stones of Ven-
ice ") that he had never seen a painted house that was
satisfactory.   Yet I suppose that he never dreamed of the
dreadful combinations which we see every day, and to
which we have not only grown resigned but callous.

ferred wooden buildings." Recently, the use of stains and the shingling of walls, especially when the shingles are left to darken naturally, have greatly improved the color-effect. Of course stone has not come into vogue except in cities, and the people, for many reasons, still prefer wood.

Pleasant Street is the main highway, with its electric line to Lynn and Salem. On the right is the Catholic Church, "The Star of the Sea," near where the roadway has been cut through a part of "Work House Rock." On this street the vagaries of Marblehead's builders soon appear. Their gable-ends encroach on the street; many of the houses have their entrance on the side, with no room for porches, but with miniature terraced gardens clambering up and spilling down over the rocks.

Near the station is a monument to the memory of the brave Captain Mugford and his heroic crew, who captured, off Boston

Harbor, a British ship laden with sorely needed military stores, including fifteen hundred barrels of gunpowder and one thousand carbines.   It was on a beautiful day in May, 1776, when, after sending in his prize to Washington's needy army, the brave patriot was killed while defending his ship against an attack by the British.   Just one hundred years after, this monument was erected.

At the Universalist Church, Rockaway Street falls abruptly to a hollow, beyond which rise the four Hooper houses with their terraced back gardens, and, above them all, the tower of Abbot Hall.   This is a typical view and street.   On the left, is Summer Street, old-fashioned and quiet, its quaint garden gates overhung by trees and flowers.   Near its end is St. Michael's, the third Episcopal Church in Massachusetts, and the fourth in all New England. Originally the church had, so it is said, seven gables, a tower, and spires, and must, as Drake says, have been an antique gem.

St. Michael's.

Not long ago it was hidden by jostling
neighbors rising in wooden chaos on all
sides, and had to be approached by a narrow

lane. Before it now is a little green, but of prodigal dimensions, for Marblehead. A tiny God's Acre is at its side, hemmed in by crowding walls. The church was built in 1714. Its interior, with quaint antiquities, is worth seeing. Rev. David Mosson, who performed the marriage ceremony of George Washington and Mrs. Custis, was once its pastor. Its organ came from St. Paul's, New York, and was used there when Washington was inaugurated, in 1789.

The Lee Mansion is reached by turning to the right, and keeping around the corner. It is now occupied by two banks ; but it was once the grand house of the town, and has sheltered Washington, Lafayette, Andrew Jackson, and President Monroe. The hall and staircase are interesting examples of the architecture of the time in which it was built — about 1766. Colonel Lee, its owner, was then the great man of Marblehead. Though a zealous churchman, who might naturally have been expected to

favor the Tories, he nevertheless was an
ardent patriot, and gave his fortune and his
life to the cause of liberty. Open-air expos-

Lee Mansion.

ure at Arlington, the night before the Battle
of Lexington, brought on a sickness from
which he finally died.

At the top of the hill is Abbot Hall,

built in 1876–77, with money left by Benjamin Abbot, a native. It contains reading rooms, a library, and some interesting paintings. Its spire dominates the town and commands a magnificent view. Before the porch, a quiet old common dozes under its elms.

Behind the Hall, Tucker Street tumbles down the hill between irregular old houses, packed in like sardines, but still finding room for little plots of sea-brightened flowers : old-fashioned dahlias, bachelors' buttons, spotted tiger lilies, asters, and petunias. A glimpse of the harbor, the rocks, and cottages of the Neck over sweet peas and clambering vines in the tiny front yards; then a turn to the right, and again one to the left, and at the bottom of the hill is Front Street, long and rambling. Along its length the houses stand at almost every angle; and the yards are as picturesque as the houses. All is enveloped in a pot pourri of marine smells from oakum, tar, pitch, and fish, its saltiness strangely attenuated at times by a whiff of

Front Street.

perfume from the gardens.   On the left,
encroaching on the street, is the
old Tucker house, the oldest house

" The backyards are as picturesque as the streets."

here of which there is any accurate record.
Beyond is State Street ; from that leads

Glover Street to General Glover's house, apparently at its end; but Glover Street continues to Front Street, so that there is no need of turning back.

Numbered 96, nearly opposite the blacksmith shop but quite a way back from the street, is the house of the General's brother, Colonel Glover. This old mansion has been divided into two tenements. It is further shorn of its dignity, for it used to stand in a great garden edged formally with box, perfumed by old-fashioned roses, and splendid with broad sunflowers and stately holly-hocks, and on either side of its gate two high posts upheld each a gilded eagle, so that it was called the Eagle House.

Twisting and turning, in and out, up and down, Front Street reaches Oakum Bay, at the end of the electric street railway. Now these street-cars do not in the least make the spot prosaic to me. Ponderous and shrilly complaining, impelled by a formless, unseen, and death-dealing energy, they seem

Tucker House.

in no wise unfitting visitors from the city of
witchcraft to this shore which for so long
echoed the despair of "The shrieking woman
of Marblehead."

Thus the legend. — Two centuries and
more ago, when the sun-blackened, scarred,
and crime-etched faces of buccaneers from
the Spanish Main were familiar in these narrow, rugged streets, a Spanish ship, richly
laden, was brought into the harbor by her
pirate captors. Every one of the ship's company had been butchered, except a beautiful
English lady. Her they brought ashore at
Oakum Bay by night, and most foully murdered. In the silence of the dark, her heart-
rending screams were heard by the wives
and children of the absent fishermen, and
for over a hundred and fifty years, on each
anniversary of the dreadful night, the cries
for mercy of the terrified woman were re-
peated in a voice shrill, unearthly, blood-
curdling. This story was believed by the
most intelligent people of Marblehead. Chief
Justice Story "averred that he had heard

those ill-omened shrieks again and again in the still hours of the night." [1]

Looking backward from here up Circle Street, Floyd Ireson's house is seen on the right.

> "Old Floyd Ireson, for his hard heart,
> Tarred and feathered and carried in a cart
> By the women of Marblehead!"

Skipper "Flud Oirson," or properly Benjamin Ireson, "sailed away from a sinking wreck" off the Highlands of Cape Cod. His defenders claim that he was inclined to attempt the rescue of the unfortunates on the doomed craft, but that his humane disposition was overruled by the unanimous voice of his craven crew. Whatever the truth may be, there is no doubt that he suffered a most ignominious punishment. "His memory has been pilloried in verse for a crime he did not commit." [1] Nor is it the best testimony that the torture was carried out by "the

[1] Drake.

Pirates in Marblehead.

women of Marblehead."[1] However, if the
fish-wives of his day were true descendants
of the old settlers, they were quite capable
of such savagery; for we have the testimony of Increase Mather, "in a letter to
Mr. Cotton, 23d of Fifth month, 1677,"
that "Sabbath day was sennight, the women
of Marblehead, *as they came out of the
meeting-house*, fell upon two Indians that
were brought in as captives, and, in a
tumultuous way, very barbarously murdered
them."

We read, too, that later on, over in Beverly, in 1777: "About 60 women marched in
regular order to the wharves, and seized a
quantity of sugar which merchants had re-
fused to sell at staple prices by reason of
depreciated currency."

[1] Mr. Roads says, by men and boys he was tarred and
feathered and dragged through the town in a dory. The
bottom fell out at Work House Rock (see page 71) and he
was then put in a cart and hauled as far as Salem, where
the authorities forbid the rabble entrance.

In a letter to Mr. Roads, Whittier writes: "I knew
nothing of the particulars, and the narrative of the ballad
was pure fancy."

The women of the North Shore were doubt-
less worthy mates for their rough husbands.

Front Street follows around Oakum Bay
to Old Fort Sewall, about which is a delightful walk. Back of the fort, on the western
slope of the hill overlooking Little Harbor,
stood the lowly cottage in which Agnes Surriage lived before fortune called her to
the Fountain Inn, there to meet the young
nobleman whose love was to raise her through
joy and sorrow, sin and repentance, so far
above her childhood's condition.

The site of the old hostelry is reached by
returning on Front Street to Franklin Street.
At the end of the latter four streets meet,
and the one at the right, Orne Street, winds
by picturesque old houses and corners to the
old burying-ground. Just before reaching
the top of the hill, a path on the right leads
to two cottages, with an old-fashioned well
under the shade of some hardy apple-trees.
This is the well of the Fountain Inn; the
building itself probably stood on the corner

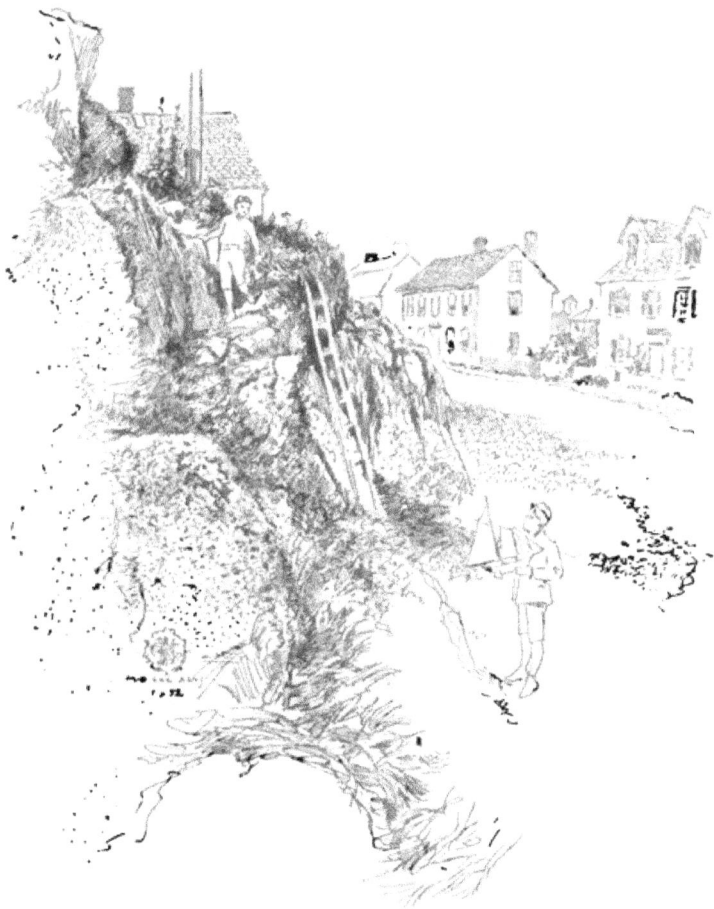

Floyd Ireson's House.

of Orne Street, and has been gone many
years. The old well was for a long time for-
gotten, and was discovered
not long ago, by chance.

Old Well of Fountain Inn.

After it was cleaned out, the water bubbled
up as clear and refreshing as ever.

The strangely romantic story of Agnes
has been told many times,[1] however I ven-

[1] See, in particular, Mr. Bynner's novel "Agnes Surriage,"
Dr. Holmes' poem "Agnes," and the Rev. Elias Mason's

ture to insert here an outline of it from the account by the Rev. Elias Mason.

It was in the summer of 1742 that Sir

Old House on the site of
the Fountain Inn.

Harry Frankland, collector of his Majesty's customs at Boston, rode up this hill and, dismounting at the Fountain Inn, chanced upon the beautiful kitchen-wench.

circumstantial and curious account, " Sir Charles Henry Frankland, Baronet."

Sir Harry meets Agnes Surriage.

" Poor Agnes! with her work half done,
  They caught her unaware,
As, humbly, like a praying nun,
  She knelt upon the stair."

The young baronet found her washing up
the floor and stairs. Ragged and dirty
clothes could not dim her radiant beauty.
She was barefoot, and he gave her, at part-
ing, a crown to buy herself some shoes and
stockings. In the autumn, Frankland came
again, and found her barefooted as before.
To his questioning, she replied that she had
indeed bought shoes and stockings with the
money given her; but that such finery she
kept to wear on Sundays only. The sweet-
ness of her voice, as he heard her cheerfully
singing at her work, her beauty, modesty,
and the sprightliness of her mind, quite cap-
tivated him; and with the consent of her
parents, he sent her to Boston to be edu-
cated. She was taught singing, dancing,
and whatever accomplishments were consid-
ered necessary to a fine lady at that time.
All this was, of course, at Frankland's ex-

pense and under his direction; for her father, a rough, ignorant fisherman, was always at his wits' ends to keep the wolf from the door.

In this self-constituted guardianship, Sir Harry and his beautiful ward, both young, were of necessity a great deal together, and a natural result followed, — they fell in love. For years, they lived together in Boston and Hopkinton. In 1754, he was called home to carry on a suit-at-law, and Agnes accompanied him. The disdain with which she was received by his noble relatives made her feel keenly the ignominy of her false position. It was therefore with pleasure that, when the occasion offered itself, they embarked for Portugal.

In the terrible earthquake at Lisbon, in 1755, Frankland was buried in the ruins, and was in great peril of his life. Happily, by the energetic devotion of his loving mistress, he was saved from a living tomb, wounded in body, but healed in mind. His conscience was quickened, and he at once repaired his wrong to Agnes by making her

Lady Frankland.

Lady Frankland.   Soon afterwards, they returned to England, where she was received
with affection and honor by his family.   She
outlived her husband, and, in 1782, was

"*Old Brig,*" *birthplace of Moll Pitcher*

married to a wealthy banker of Chichester,
England.

Across Orne Street, No. 42, is "The Old
Brig," where Moll Pitcher passed her girl-

hood. She seems to have inherited her
claim to supernatural power from her father,
John Dimond. His was a character strangely
picturesque, whether we regard him as an
impostor or a sincere believer in his own
brainsick pretensions. The historian Drake
says: "He was in the habit of going to the
old burying-ground on the hill, whenever a
violent gale at sea arose, and in that lonely
place, in the midst of the darkness and the
storm, to astound and terrify the simple
fisher-folk in the following manner. He
would direct vessels then at sea how to
weather the roughest gale, — pacing up and
down among the gravestones, and ever and
anon, in a voice distinctly heard above the
howling of the tempest, shout his orders to
the helmsman or the crew, as if he were
actually on the quarterdeck and the scene
all before him. Very few doubted his abil-
ity to bring a vessel safely into port."[1]

On the top of the hill the first church was
built, and about it the early settlers laid

[1] Drake.

their dead, in the earth-filled crevices of the rocks. The church was moved away long ago; but burial of the dead there has long been continued, perhaps to the present time.

General Glover's Tomb.

General Glover's tomb is here, and Captain Mugford's unknown grave.

At the highest point is the seamen's monument, and about it seats and a shelter. On the benches the old men sit, for they are content to rest. Their weather-beaten faces are darkened by contrast with their white beards and hair. They talk of the past, of the sea, of ships and sailors. The broad horizon of the deep is before them, and about them are the graves.

On the rugged hill across the street is Fountain Park. From its little summer-house is an unobstructed view of the harbor and bay. The slope below is littered with the picturesque belongings of the lobster men, scattered about their quaint huts. Once this shore was lined with wharves, and the hill covered with fish-flakes. Here, or upon the two little islands near by, was made the first settlement. Orne Street continues from the hill down into this oldest part of the town, which is called Barnegat. At its end is Peach's Point and the entrance to Salem Harbor. Beyond is the beautiful Beverly and Manchester shore, across a bay dotted by rocky islets and dangerous reefs that break its breeze-whipped waters into foam and spray,

white accents to its mingled blue and green
and purple. Beyond all, over bay and fort

Lobsterman's Hut.

and town and harbor, the ocean stretches
the restful monotony of its blue rim till

hidden by the roof-trees and steeples of the
old town.

Old Stone Church.

Orne Street, retraced to its beginning,
leads to Washington Street. On the right
side of the latter is the old " North Church,"
and nearly opposite is No. 44, the homestead
of Captain Thomas Gerry. In one of the old

mansion's chambers, unchanged to this day, was born the captain's distinguished son,

Elbridge Gerry's Birthplace.

Elbridge Gerry, a signer of the Declaration of Independence, and once Vice-President of the United States.

Farther on, stands, in the middle of the road, the old Town House. This is the Faneuil Hall of Marblehead, and in it the town's famous Revolutionary regiment, called the Amphibions, was recruited.

At the right of the Town Hall, Mugford Street leads up a slight rise to the Unitarian church. And just beyond the church, on the corner of Back Street, is the house in which the brave Captain Mugford set up housekeeping with his young bride. From here, agitated by her tearful embrace, he set hopefully forth on that gallant adventure, so fruitfully precious to his countrymen, and from which he was brought back dying, to receive from his young wife a last caress. It was into the house by the church, nearly opposite, that they sadly bore him; and there he breathed his last. This house was her home before marriage, and the scene of their courtship; it belonged to her father, John Griste, and has always remained in the possession of the family.

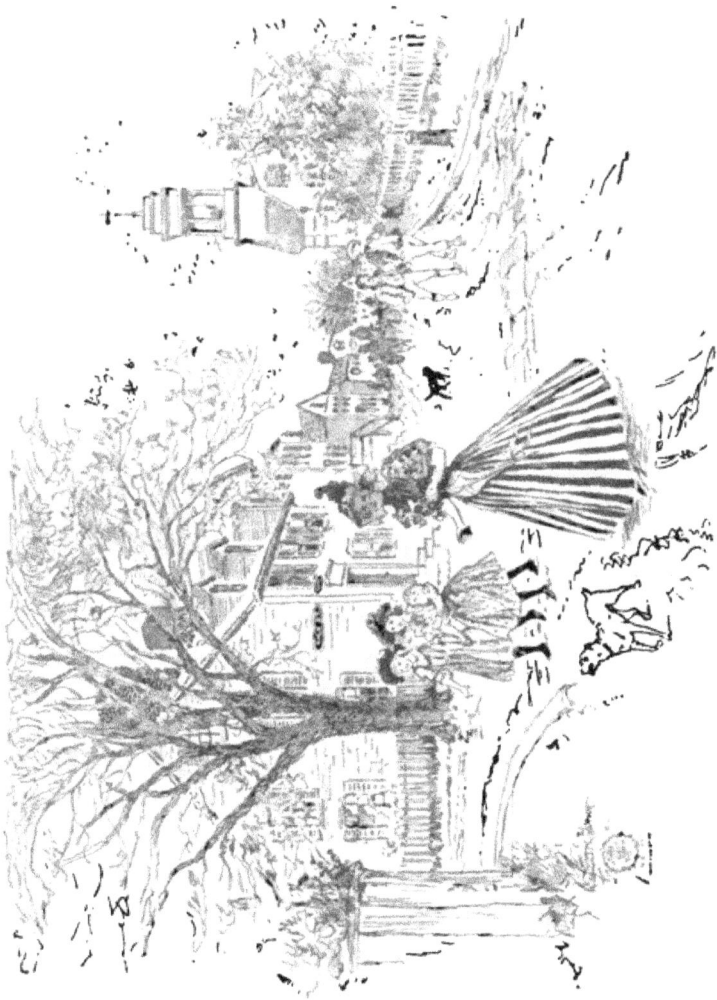

Corner of Buck and Mugford Streets.

On the corner of Elm Street is the soldiers' monument. This street may be followed to the Salem Road; but it is pleasanter to return to Washington Street, on which, just after passing the town hall on the left, is the birthplace of Judge Story. The old house has been divided, and the lower story is now used for an apothecary shop.

Pleasant Street, which is the entrance, is also the way out of this old-fashioned town, the quaintest and most antique on the coast. And though these qualities commend it to the artist and the antiquary, it must to all Americans be dear for the independence, courage, bravery, and ever-ready patriotism of its adventurous sons. On land as well as by sea, in every hour of need, they have always answered unfalteringly to their country's call.

"THE road from Salem to Marblehead, four miles, is pleasant indeed (so I found it)."

So wrote John Adams in 1776, and a hundred and twenty years afterwards it may again truly be called "pleasant indeed." All the way, by open fields and long rows of apple-trees, it is good wheeling. At the bend of the road, before it dips to Forest River, there should be a fine view over the valley; but it is cut off by a hideous blue and boastful advertising fence, with which another, a black and white conundrum, disputes dishonors.

Below the bridge, the river empties into a broad lagoon at high water, and at low water wanders off through the mud-flats to Salem Harbor. Lafayette Street, a fine drive, leads by some of the best houses to Central Street, which, as its name implies, is near the centre of the city. A statue has been raised here to that apostle of temperance, Father Mathew. It stands appropriately on the site of a spring which supplied water to the first settlers. That it was good water we know. Did not old Governor Dudley declare there was "good water to drinke till wine or beare can be made"?

The early comers would naturally have settled near some sweet fountain such as this was, until the day when they could build houses and dig wells. In fact, near by, in Charter Street, is an old witness of a time not far removed from the first settlement, — the Charter Street Cemetery, known in early days as "Burying Point."

Now, in Salem, the stranger is mostly
interested in those things connected with the
Witchcraft Delusion, or in those places made
precious by their association with the life
and work of Hawthorne. And in the old
Charter Street Burying-ground both these
interests are served, for here lies buried the
old witch-judge, Colonel John Hathorne, and
at one corner stands the Grimshaw house,
in which Hawthorne courted his wife. This
old house, practically unchanged to-day,
figures in the "Dolliver Romance," and
again in "Dr. Grimshaw's Secret," though
in no agreeable light, which seems strange
considering that Hawthorne here won his
wife, and that his memories must have been
far removed from the gloomy pictures of
his romance. Its garden fence is close
to the oldest graves, with their quaint,
mouldering headstones and curious epitaphs.
Here lies "Dr. John Swinnerton, Physi-
cian," who appears in "The House of the
Seven Gables," and again as the ancient
apothecary at the sign of "The Brazen Ser-

pent " in the " Dolliver Romance." Near
by is the grave of Cotton Mather's younger
brother Nathaniel, " ' An aged man at nine-
teen years,' saith the gravestone." Here
was buried Giles Corey's first wife, and
in the cemetery are also buried " Governor Bradstreet, Chief Justice Lynde, and
others, whose virtues, honors, courage, and
sagacity have nobly illustrated the history
of Salem."

Essex Street, Salem's principal thorough-
fare, is reached by Liberty Street. From
the corner of these two streets, a half
block to the left, is the East India Marine
Hall, containing extensive collections of
historical portraits, natural history and eth-
nological specimens, and curiosities of many
kinds.

Nearly opposite the corner of Liberty, on
the other side of Essex Street, are the Cadet
Armory, Plummer Hall, the Salem Athenæum,
and the Essex Institute. The last holds collections of paintings, prints, cooking utensils,

household implements, weapons, pottery,
china, coins, and many other objects of interest.[1]   In the rear of the Institute is the frame
of the first Puritan house of worship in the
New World. It may be visited on applica-
tion to the secretary.

The third street on the right beyond the
Institute is Union Street. In the modest
gambrel-roofed house now numbered 27,
Nathaniel Hawthorne, the great romancer,
was born.   The house was built before the
witch-craft delusion, and came into the possession of the novelist's grandfather in 1772.
The house itself is little changed since Hawthorne's birth ; but it then stood in a garden,
and what is now arid and unattractive was
sweet with blade and leaf and blossom. Staid
and Sabbath like quiet brooded over its grass-
edged precincts, and its ways were ordered
by New England thrift and neatness.   It is
hard now to re-invest the place with that old-

---

[1] Visitors should buy the "Guide to Salem," published by the Institute; the author is largely indebted
to it.

time charm. Too near and evident is the
untidy ash-barrel, too pungent the odorous
herring and cabbage, too distracting the

Hawthorne's Birthplace

shrill quarrel and grating discord of clamorous hucksters. It is only afterwards, and in
the mind's eye, that it is possible to connect
the to-day's fallen estate with the coming of
that dreaming weaver of romance.

Numbered 10½ and 12 on Herbert Street,
the next street leading from Essex Street,
and back of Hawthorne's birthplace, is the

The Manning Homestead.

old Manning homestead, the property of his
grandfather, and to which his widowed mother
removed in 1808, when Nathaniel was four

years old. Most of his boyhood was spent
here ; and he came back to it, at intervals, for
longer or shorter visits. The house is outwardly square and ugly, and the interior has
been cut up into tenements. However, it is
of great interest, on account of its association with his early work. Hawthorne's room
was in the southwest corner of the third story,
overlooking his birthplace. Of it, he himself
has written : " Here I sit in my old accus-
tomed chamber, where I used to sit in days
gone by. Here I have written many tales.
Should I have a biographer, he ought to
make great mention of this chamber in my
memoirs, because so much of my lonely
youth was wasted here." And again : " In
this dismal chamber FAME was won."

At the other end of Herbert Street is
Derby Street, and on the corner is a house
to which Hawthorne was always welcome,
where he spent a part of his time in a chamber kept ever ready for him, and in which,
and in the old garden, he wrote some of his
earlier stories. Antique and dilapidated, it

is one · of the most picturesque houses in
Salem ; for the summer-house, where the

Where Hawthorne was
always welcome.

romancer loved to sit, is tumbling to pieces,
and the garden is forlorn in its neglect. All
sorts of weeds grow rankly in its wastes, and

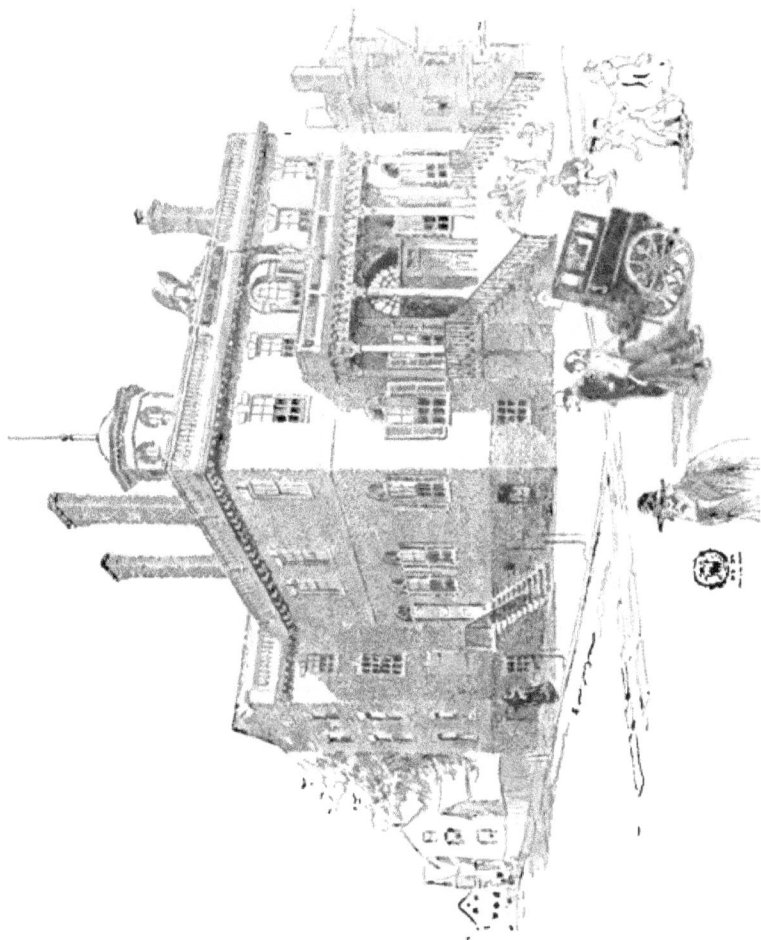

The Custom House.

a little thicket of crowding poplars nearly
hides, with the gray silver of their leaves,
the purple and white of the ancient lilacs and
the weather-beaten grays of the lower story.

At No. 180 Derby Street, is the Crown-
inshield house, in the eastern side of which
lived General James Miller, the hero of Lundy's
Lane. On the opposite corner is the custom-
house, built of brick, with wooden columns,
capitals, and balustrades, with a broad red-
flagged sidewalk, and generous steps and
porch. The gilded "truculent bird" still
perches aloft, and "the flag with vertical
bars" still floats over all. Hawthorne's room
is shown here; but the desk on which he
scratched his name is now at the Essex
Institute. One of the upper rooms is the
scene of his fictitious discovery of the em-
broidered scarlet letter, and his interview
with the spook of Surveyor Pue.

Across the street, is the old custom-house
wharf, edged with sheds in various stages
of decrepitude and disuse. Under their

leaky roofs I saw some old horse-cars that were cast away. They had, in their youth, supplanted the stage-coaches in which Hawthorne's relatives were financially interested, and now they were in turn displaced by the electric cars. Here they were rotting and rusting away like those very stage-coaches in which Hawthorne used to play when he was a boy. And fast to the wharf lay a great dismantled ship, the " Mindora," only a caretaker aboard. She paid for herself on the first voyage, but after thirty years of service, the competition of steam had so lowered freights that it no longer was expedient to send her to sea, and so she lies here inactive, to deteriorate, as everything inactive must.[1] The long wharf curves at the end, like the beak of " the truculent bird," and at its end is a little light-house. Across the harbor, the shore of Marblehead stretches northeasterly to Naugus Head, and landward lies the dreary water front of Salem.

[1] Early in 1897 the " Mindora " was sold and towed away to be altered over into a coal-barge.

Hawthorne and the wraith of Collector Pue.

Farther down Derby Street is Turner Street,
on which is an old house that belonged to

Old Custom House Wharf.

the Ingersols, relatives of the Hawthornes,
a house to which the romancer was a fre-

quent visitor. It is the last dwelling on the
right, and next the Seaman's Bethel. This
house is called "The House of the Seven
Gables." Originally it had five gables, but
they have disappeared under a new roof.
Its exterior seems modern enough, but a
visit to the inside will show that it is truly
very old. The old gables may be traced in
the attic; parts of the house are pointed out,
which, it is claimed, agree with the story.
Really the house may have had but a small
part in suggesting to Hawthorne his fanciful
"House of the Seven Gables," but it is so
closely associated with the author's intimate
life, that it is worth a visit.

Turner Street leads back to Essex Street,
and from the latter turns Washington Square,
East, which bounds one side of the large and
pleasant common, cut by paths and malls,
and shaded by beautiful trees. Many of the
great elms were planted in 1802, and the
common was then used as a training-field
by the militia. It is the pleasantest resting-
spot in Salem.

After turning into Washington Square,
North, the third street on the right is Mall
Street. On the corner is a curious old-
fashioned double house used for a curiosity
shop. These abound in Salem; in fact, if
antiques do not represent a local industry,
as some mockers hint, they are no incon-
siderable article of the city's trade.

A short distance down Mall Street, No. 14,
on the right, is a comfortable hip-roofed
house standing with end to the street, and
shaded by trees in its pleasant garden.
This is one of the most interesting houses
in Salem, for in it was written "The Scarlet Letter," the masterpiece by which the
world best knows, and will longest remember Hawthorne. He moved here in 1847,
and his study was the front room in the third
story.

When he lost his office in the customs, "it
was to this house he went home to tell the
serious news to his wife. It was here, upon
learning it, that she said, 'Very well! now
you can write your romance;' and it was

here that his prudent wife at the same time,
and in answer to Hawthorne's query as to
how they should live meanwhile, opened the
bureau-drawer and showed him the gold she

House in which "The Scarlet Letter" was written.

had saved from the portion of his salary
which, from time to time, he had placed in
her hands. . . . Here Fields found Hawthorne, despondent and hovering near the
stove, and had the interesting conversation

with him given in Fields' 'Yesterdays with Authors.'"

Brown Street issues from Washington Square, West, and on the corner of it and St. Peter's Street is St. Peter's church. It is a pleasant ivy-clad, stone edifice with a square tower, rising between two tiny church-yards. In the one on the right, close by the fence, is the grave of Hawthorne's ghostly visitor: "Jonathan Pue, Esq., Late surveyor and searcher of his magestie's customs in Salem, New England."

The church is modern, having been built in 1833. Within is a tablet "In memory of John Brown, to whose intrepidity in the Cause of Religious Freedom, this the first Episcopal Society gathered in N. E., under God, owed its establishment in 1629, and to Philip English who gave the land." This last gentleman was one of the accused in the Witchcraft Delusion. He and his wife were both denounced, and only escaped death by fleeing to New York from Boston jail, with the connivance of Governor Sir William

Phips, and especially aided by the Reverend Joshua Moody. After the town's madness had passed away, Mr. English and his wife returned to Salem, where Mrs. English died from the effects of the cruel treatment she had received. It is a satisfaction to learn that Mr. Moody "was commended by all discerning men;" but nevertheless so greatly was he persecuted by the angry and resentful multitude, that he returned to his old charge at Portsmouth, N. H.

Farther down St. Peter's Street is a very old house, built in 1684 by John Ward, sometimes incorrectly called the Waller house.

Church Street is almost a continuation of Brown Street, and leads to Washington Street, where stood the court-house in which the witchcraft trials were held. On a bronze tablet, near the corner of Lynde Street, are set forth the main facts of that unhappy delusion. The hotel on this street occupies a very old mansion with a quaintly-decorated cupola, which may be visited.

Near the present centre of Washington
Street, the Town House Square of to-day,
stood the town pump celebrated by Hawthorne. The well dried up after the railway
tunnel was built.

The oldest house in Salem or vicinity is
the " Old Witch House," once owned by
Roger Williams; it is No. 310 Essex Street,
at the corner of North Street. Though
changed a great deal, some parts of it
remain as they were, including the old
chimney in the rear of the drug-store. The
truth is, that it has been connected with the
witchcraft delusion by tradition only. However, if one wishes to see a house whose
connection with that gruesome time is un-
doubted, let him examine the house No. 315
Essex Street, which is little changed, and
was the home of the dyer, Shattuck, whose
child was said to have been bewitched by
Bridget Bishop.

In this direction is Gallows' Hill, but there
is really nothing to see there. I went there
years ago, to make a drawing for Longfellow's

"New England Tragedies," and I confess
that I have never gone again. The witchcraft tragedy is an unpleasant subject, whenever it is approached with the seriousness it
must deserve from any but the most thought-
less; but, except to the historian or philoso-
pher, it must claim only a morbid interest.
It is better to think of Salem's commercial
achievements, her patriotism and philan-
thropy, and to visit her museums, her libra-
ries and schools.

BEVERLY is reached by returning to Washington Square, North, and following Winter and Bridge streets to Essex Bridge. A refreshing breeze generally draws up the river from the sea, flecks the bay with white, and sings mournfully a long monotony in the wires overhead. Though the view on both sides is fine, that up the river is marred by the railway causeway. Across the bay, "The Willows" is cheerful with flags and music, and the old fort peaceful in decay. In the harbor are mingled picturesquely sail-boats and yachts, their slender spars and snowy canvas contrasted with the dingy sails of rusty coasters and grimy, clumsy coal-barges.

Just across the bridge, Cabot Street leads to Front Street, and at No. 22 of the latter is an old house, once used as a church, in which in 1810 was established the first Sunday-school in America. Bartlett and Stone Streets then lead to Lothrop Street, a famous drive, overlooking the sea. Only a little way down the latter is a pleasant resting-place in a little summer-house; it stands at the head of three flights of steps descending to the beach. Shady and cool, it commands a broad view of Beverly Cove and the mouth of Salem Harbor.

When I last rested here, an old man was sitting contentedly on one of the benches. He told me that he sailed into Beverly Cove for the first time when he was fourteen years old, in a coaster from Maine. "And," he

added, "that was seventy-nine years ago."
He liked, so he said, to come here and watch
the water and the vessels, for, having always
followed the sea, he was lonesome and uneasy

Beverly Cove.

when away from it. He named the islands
to me, starting from the left over Wood-
bury's Point. First, came Great and Little
Misery, but these seemed almost a part of

the mainland; then Baker's, with its twin
lights; and nearer, Great Haste and Coney,
islets both; and farther off, between them,
Eagle Island, on which fat gooseberries used
to grow; and last, over against Salem Neck,
Lowell's Island, with its institution. I
asked him whether, in his time, these islands
had ever been wooded. He answered that
they were bare when he first saw them (1817),
and that in his boyhood, old men, as old as
he was now, could not remember having ever
seen any trees upon them.

So the islands must have been cleared a
long time ago. Wooded they were, for the
Rev. Francis Higginson wrote in his journal
in June, 1629:—

"Monday, 29th, as we passed along to Naim-
keake [*i. e.*, Salem] it was wonderful to behold so
many islands replenished with thicke wood and
high trees, and many fayere green pastures."

In the cove, many coasters were anchored.
The old sailor said that most of them had
been there several days, that they expected

the equinoctial, and were therefore afraid to
trust themselves off a lee shore, and though
in their present anchorage they were exposed
to the winds, they would ride in safety
there, for the reefs and islands broke all the
force of the seas. So the rocks shelter as
well as destroy.

He also told me that he would rather be
cast away on rocks than on sand; and he
instanced two wrecks, — one at Gloucester,
where a vessel had come on the rocks, and
the crew had crawled ashore, over the bow-
sprit; the other at Swampscott, where "every
soul, including a cat and dog," just walked
out on the jibboom, and dropped right down
into the road. When a vessel goes on the
sands, however, almost every one is surely
lost.

There is a long coast from here to some
fine willows and a fountain, by a lane leading to the other end of the beach, beyond
which the first turn to the right leads to
Ober Street, and thence by Neptune and

Bay View streets, to Paul's Head. These
streets are much like English lanes, and for
one in love with beauty it is no place to
hurry.

Instead of disfiguring the landscape, as
they too often do, the houses add to it a pic-

Paul's Head.

turesque feature, standing as they do amid
velvety lawns and banks of flowers, and separated from the road by vine-clad walls or
beautiful shrubs and hedges. Under green
oaks and maples their gardens overhang the
sea in unexpected variety.

White with the dazzling white which only whitewash can give, and beside which all other whites are gray, the square prim lighthouse tower enhances and deepens the blue of sky and bay. The keeper's home is a châlet-like cottage, from whose walls slope the grassy banks, pretty with flowers, down to the rocky shore. What a contrast is the berth here to one in the wave-shaken tower on Minot's Ledge, or in an ever-tossing lightship over some lonely shoals!

Before returning to the road, it is interesting to look up the old breastworks back of the lighthouse; for this point was fortified during the Revolution, and the esplanade just beyond the light, and now divided amongst fine estates, was, during the struggle with the mother country, a great training ground and camp for the colonists.

The first turn to the right, after the road has been retraced a little, leads by Neptune Street to Hale Street. It is good wheeling, but out of sight of the sea.   However, after turning to the right, by the blacksmith-shop at Chapman's Corner, the street suddenly enters a stretch of woodland exquisitely beautiful.

At times the road is so shadowed by the splendid overhanging trees that only here and there is it flecked by narrow shafts of sunshine which have struggled through the leafy screen.   Paths and driveways lead, discreetly and furtively, to foliage-hidden houses.   The trees rise high above tumbled rocks and bowlders.   From the covert of ferns and sombre depths of shade, they lift their trunks and branches to the sun.   This is the edge of the famous Witch Woods, thus named because it is so hard to find one's way that they were believed to be bewitched.

The early settlers held these woods in great fear, believing them infested by lions at least, if not worse!   The author of "New England's Prospect," though he admits that he himself had never seen any lions, de-

clares, quaintly, that "Some likewise, being
lost in the woods, have heard such terrible
roarings, as have made them much aghast;
which must be either devils or lions; there
being no other creatures which use to roar,
saving bears, which have not such a terrible
kind of roaring." But to-day, the edge of
the forest seems more like a delightful park
than the lair of savage beasts, clawed or
cloven of foot, and, so cleverly has it all
been arranged, that its sylvan character is
not lost, nor is the presence of the near
estates too keenly felt.

As I caught, now and then, a glimpse of
some fine house, or passed the rolling carriages and other evidences of Beverly's
wealth, I recalled with amusement the petition to the General Court, in 1671, of the
venerable Roger Conant, "who hath bin a
planter in New England fortie yeers and
upwards," praying that the name be changed
from Beverly to that of his native town,
Budleigh, and giving as his first and prin-

cipal reason "the great dislike and discontent of many of our people for this name of Beverly, because (we being a small place) it hath caused on us a constant nickname of Beggarly!" The petition was not granted, and time has taken away Roger Conant's cause of complaint.

A regret will come, sometimes, that one is so shut off from the shore; and one reverts mentally to the open freedom of the cliff at Newport; but the road soon winds back, or the shore curves in, and suddenly there rises the sea's edge; the bay and islands follow. It is the famous view over Mingo Beach.

The first sight of any celebrated view is apt to be disappointing. Either zest is dulled and pleasure discounted by anticipation, or overpraise has raised too great an expectancy. This view at Mingo Beach, for example, has been often compared to that of the Bay of Naples; yet all they have in common is that beauty of sky and water to

be expected in a common latitude. The
shores themselves have no resemblance.

Mingo Beach.

Nothing could be more unlike the steep
volcanic slopes of Naples,

" Where the waves and mountains meet,"

than these low, wooded shores. Lowell's
and Baker's islands do not remind one of

Ischia and Capri, whose craggy precipices
tower over two thousand feet above the sea.
Think, too, of Monte Sant' Angelo, rising
abruptly from Castelmare, nearly a mile,
while, above buried Herculaneum and Pom-
peii, Vesuvius hangs her white wreath of
smoke, and Naples rears her hills, topped by
mediæval castles.   Through the burning
mountain, Nature speaks of past destruction,
and ever menaces the future.   The frowning
castles and towers recite man's long struggle
against oppression and cruelty, kingcraft and
priestcraft, his fight for liberty, security, and
happiness.   And the stern spirit of all this
is shared by our shores as well as the common beauty.   If the volcano is more terrible,
it is no fiercer than the treacherous sea,
which yearly exacts its tribute of death.
Even the name of the beach here perpetuates
the memory of slavery.[1]   Salem, like Naples,
has been scourged by cruelty and supersti-
tion.   The people must ever struggle against

[1] It is named after a negro slave of Beverly, Robin
Mingo.

greed and oppression, which only change
their form, not their nature. But outwardly
the shore has an appearance, almost bour-
geois, of restful peace, comfort, and
prosperity.

Comparisons should be carefully made, for
they will arise; they are our only measures.
As I leaned over the wall here, at the close
of a calm afternoon, the blue sea barely
wrinkled by the afternoon breeze, reminded
me of the Mediterranean. Surely, it was
quite as blue; for our idea of that vaunted
sea abroad has come to us through the praises
in English prose and verse. Heavenly blue
it must seem to British eyes, used to the
gray and yellow seas of the Channel, or
the cold North Sea, over which "Go rolling
the storm-clouds, the formless, dark, gray
daughters of the air."

But one sea must not be lauded at the ex-
pense of another. Each has its particular
individual beauty. And this same gray
North Sea I have known the quintessence of
sunlight. Once, from a steamer's deck, I

had been watching the coast of Holland, a
mother-of-pearl horizon over the white-
capped sea, when suddenly the ship slowed
down and I crossed to the port side.   Over
the bow was Flushing, its walls drenched and
belabored by the dashing surf, that broke
into great sheets of spray and went flying
over the walls into the streets and windows,
and onto the very roofs.   The sun flashed
on the waves in almost painful brilliancy,
and the sea was all yellow and white; and
over this heaving yellow sea came a pilot-
boat, yellow too, with a tawny sail, and
manned by a crew all in yellow oilskins
(except one harmoniously green), and all
drenched and flashing in the day beams and
sparkling foam, — a glorious symphony in
yellow, and the keenest expression of sunlight I have ever seen.

As for blue and green, the Mediterranean
and our own sea are but as ashes, when compared to the azure and emerald glowing over
the coral sands and ledges of Bermuda,

" By bays, the peacock's neck in hue."

Our own sea, like the Mediterranean or any other, follows the changes of the sky, and so it runs the subtle scale of cloudy grays, the rosy, silvery morning tints, all the yellows and reds of sunset, and the sombre tones of night. Still it is often an intense blue, deepened to purple over sunken reefs, and enhanced by emerald pools over patches of sand.

Yes, as I said, it was very blue that calm afternoon. On the horizon rested a low bank of clouds, like distant fog, and above it, the sky melted through changing opalescent color into deep azure. South of the zenith, hung the moon, nearly full, but pale and faint. The incoming yachts caught the yellowing rays of the sun, and slowly made the harbor. Only the sound of faintly splashing water rose from the warm-toned rocks below; no sound of voices broke the decorous quiet of the road. Occasionally, came the rumble of carriages, the impact of hoofs, or the soft purr of a coasting wheel. As the sun dropped lower, all the east glowed with reflected glory, — sea, shore, and sky echoed the west; Color and Light, the two great magicians,

Catholic Church.

transmuted our familiar coast and bay into a slowly fading loveliness, as night came on.

One turns away regretfully from such beauty. Farther on, the way is less interesting, and at Pride's crosses the railway, and again at Beverly Farms, three-quarters of a

"*Beverly-by-the-Depot.*"

mile beyond. On the way is Emerson's pretty Catholic church by vine-hung cottages, which together make a picturesque note. Just before reaching the Farms' station, last on the right, is the house once occupied by Oliver

Wendell Holmes, and from which he dated
his letters, "Beverly-by-the-Depot," in emu-
lation of Manchester-by-the-Sea.   Nearly opposite, in the last house on the left, square
and old-fashioned, once lived Lucy Larcom.
We have her own testimony that it was on
this road between Marblehead and Beverly
that she used to see, sitting wistfully at the
window, "Hannah, binding shoes."   Not
quite here, however, for it must have been
somewhere in sight of the sea —

> " May is passing, —
> Mid the apple-boughs a pigeon coos.
> Hannah shudders,
> For the wild sou'wester mischief brews.
> Round the rocks of Marblehead,
> Outward bound, a schooner sped :
> Silent, lonesome,
> Hannah 's at the window binding shoes.
>
> "'T is November :
> Now no tear her wasted cheek bedews.
> From Newfoundland
> Not a sail returning will she lose ;
> Whispering hoarsely, ' Fishermen,
> Have you, have you heard of Ben ? '
> Old with watching,
> Hannah 's at the window binding shoes.

> " Twenty winters
> Bleach and tear the rugged shore she views ;
> Twenty seasons ; —
> Never one has brought her any news !
> Still her dim eyes silently
> Chase the white sails o'er the sea.
> Hopeless, faithful,
> Hannah 's at the window binding shoes."

After crossing the railway, the road comes
quickly to the head of West Beach.   At low

West Beach.

water, its sands offer a long stretch of good
wheeling, and, by going a little back towards
Beverly, a good view may be had of the
picturesque coast and islands of Manchester.

Manchester

BEYOND West Beach, the road crosses the railway again, and leaves the sea for the woods. Black Cove and Tuck's Point may be visited by taking the first turn to the right. At Tuck's Point is the yacht club-house and a fine public pier jutting out from a little park. A maze of inlets and islands seams the harbor from the pier's end. It is worth the détour, both for the view of the cove and harbor, and the pleasant ride through the lanes coming and going.

The way back is to the right by Harbor Street, over the railway bridge, and again to

the right, when Bridge Street is reached.
From this corner it is only half a mile to

Tuck's Point.

Manchester, once an ancient fishing-port
and a part of Salem, now a quiet, typical
New England village.

Church, school-house, town hall, and inn
are all gathered about the village green, in
the middle of which is a fine granite fountain.
There are not many ancient houses; but the
general appearance is one of peaceful and
prosperous age. The meeting·house in the
square was built in 1809, and has a quaint
and very graceful belfry and steeple. The
weathercock was provided by the town in
1754, at a cost of £7 10s. 8d., for the old
church which the present structure super-
seded.

The proposal to heat this church on Sundays was firmly opposed by many of the con-
gregation, says the local historian. In the
end, the party of progress was too strong for
the remonstrants, and it was announced
from the pulpit one Sunday, that thereafter
the church would be heated on the Lord's
Day. During worship on the next Sabbath,
many were overcome by the heat, several
women fainted, and others had to leave the
church for a breath of fresh air. It is fair
to presume that these afflicted ones were of

the opposition, for after service it was discovered that, owing to a defect in the heater,
no fire had been started that morning.

Manchester Public Library and Church.

Around the corner, on Union
Street, is the Memorial Public
Library given to the town by
the Hon. T. Jefferson Coolidge.   It contains
interesting old wood-carvings and memorial

tablets. In addition to the Memorial hall
and library, it has a hall for the use of the
G. A. R.

The next street to the right crosses the

Manchester Harbor.

railway, passes the head of the harbor, and
mounts the hill to Masconomo Road, hard
by the great hotel. The red and gambrel-
roofed house, high upon Thunderbolt Rock,

at the right was the
summer home of James
T. Fields.

One should now turn
to the right, pass the
Unitarian chapel, and
keep on down the quiet English-like lane
by the pretty Episcopal church with its

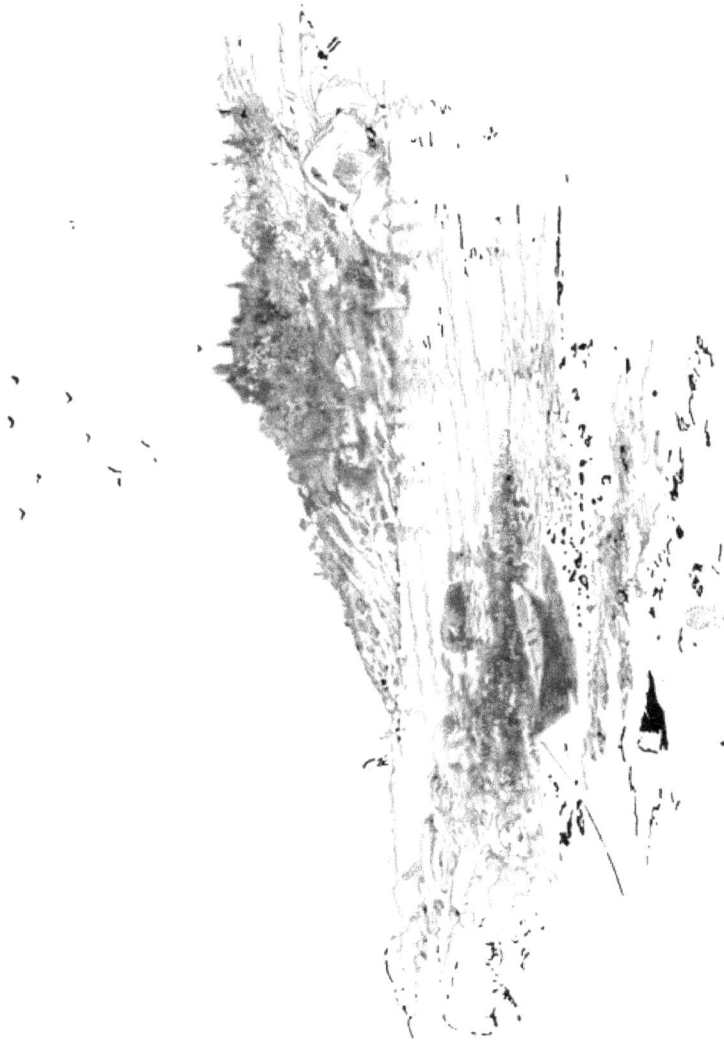

Lobster Cove.

vines and picturesque lich-gate, to the shore
of Lobster Cove.

This little nook, sheltered by rocky points,
is overlooked by châlet and castle-like houses
in admirable harmony with their surround-
ings. It is one of the prettiest spots on the
coast. The narrow lane separates the beach
from a gem-like
pond. On one side
is the kelp-strewn,
rock-buttressed
beach and the sea,
sparkling like
spangled cobalt
under the sun.
The tide softly laps the flat stones. A hundred feet distant from its brine is the fresh
water of the little pond, fringed with grass,
and dotted with lily-pads and arrow-heads.
Under the autumn breeze its rippled surface
takes on a blue deeper than ultramarine,
and is all ringed about by an indescribable
tangle of reddening and bronzing shrubs and
vines.

Gnarled trees and jagged rocks overhang the shady lane, where it climbs the hill over Gale's Point.   Here is a lesson in landscape-gardening, for the noble estates are an added charm to the natural beauty.   Over the lawn open glimpses of the sea, framed by trees and vines.

From a little summer-house on the hill's top, there is an extended view of great charm.   Over the deep azure of the bay, beyond faint Nahant, rise the pearly blue hills of Milton; nearer, lies Marblehead, "Its porphyry promontories sleeping in the sun;" then Salem, between the white sails in Beverly Cove and the purple ridges of Lynn Woods; then the shimmering sands of West Beach and the rocky wooded shore, seen between the odd-shaped roofs, as it swings into the harbor, and on to where the little white belfry dominates all but the water tower on Powder House Hill.   Then come green rolling hills, until, in the east, the ocean again raises its high wall to the sky.

The Shady Lane.

It is only a little way back to the Masconomo House, where Beach Street descends
to Singing Beach. Perhaps the first thing
to arrest the attention is not the musical
accomplishments of the shore, but rather the
rich coloring of its sands, — for it is quite

Eagle's Head from Singing Beach.

unlike the beaches that have been passed.
In texture, more like the sand of Cape Cod,
it is ruddy and beautiful, — a warm tawny
pink in sunlight, which fairly glows against
the dark background of the sea. However,
its "singing" is really its great attraction.
Underfoot, it seemed to me like the crisp

little note that the snow gives out in very cold weather; and under carriage-wheels, like the long-continued tone a heavy sleigh draws from a frosty snow-packed road.

The beach ends at the left in a rocky promontory called Eagle Head, that is well rusted by wind and spray, where it shows a bare beak to the sea; but landward it is feathered with straggling green.

From the beach, the way must be retraced to Sea Street, which will bring one to Summer Street, the Gloucester Road. Just opposite the corner is an old burying-ground (1661), under a thick grove of pines which seem to rise from the very graves. Close by the sunny highway, these grimly nurtured trees cast a sombre shadow, broken only by the deeper sadness of their black trunks. Strangely uneven is the ground, and heavily carpeted with pine-needles. It seems unsafe to walk upon, — yielding like some unnatural quicksand. The marble slabs are stained green or smooched with black, and their elders, the old slate headstones, lean de-

crepitly, or seem sinking wearily down into
the graves.

Just beyond the graveyard, a quaint sign-
post points the way to the grounds of the
Essex County Club. From here on, the road
is uninteresting until the brick-yards are past,
and one enters the Manchester Woods.

On either side of the way, then, is romantic, sylvan beauty. From the serious mystery
of their covert, the straight trunks rise slen-
derly through a maze of leafy branches. In
the hollow where the brook trickles the soil,
in midsummer, is thick-hid by brakes and
ferns; but on the climbing bank at the other
side, patches of warm brown and gray show
where the rocky ground rises toward the sea.
At the left, the woods overhang, and the
tracery of trees and saplings is drawn against
tumbled rocks and ledges, or broad dashes of
golden-green where a shaft of sunshine has
pierced a group of maples. Rock-strewn, a
subtle harmony of gray and green, are the
gullies near the top of the hill, enamelled

with silvery lichens and mosses in tint varying from emerald to olive black.

Black Beach and Manchester Cove.

After emerging from these woods, Ocean
Street, the first right, runs down the hill to a
pretty little beach, and turning to the left,
skirts Manchester Cove, on the other side of
which is Coolidge's Point.   The waters of

the cove invade the meadows at the left, and
the flood-tide, rushing tumultuously under
the bridge, brims to overflowing the winding
river. Along its placid curves the country is
much like parts of England. The hills are
embowered in softly rounded foliage, and in
its rich green shelter lie tilled fields, fruitful
orchards, and trim cottages. On a calm
evening, with the sunset light over the hills
and reflected in the river, and all detail
blended and massed under the gathering
twilight, the sentiment of the scene is one of
profound peace.

The shingly beach and the meadow-edge
are littered with dories, nets, anchors, and
all the picturesque belongings of fishermen.
Most of the travel is on the highway, so that
one generally has this road almost to one's
self. As I stood here one beautiful October
day, the smoke of autumn fires drifted lazily
over the harvested fields. The goldenrod
had lost its flaming yellow, and deliciously
brown in tone, harmonized wonderfully well
with the lavender-purple asters and the straw-

yellow of the grass. Toward Magnolia, the purple rocks on the hills shouldered aside the red and bronzed bushes, sombre and rich as antique rugs. The breeze was a little chilly, but in warm, sheltered spots a few bees still hummed, and long-bodied wasps crawled about the path where gorgeous green and golden flies sunned themselves, and buzzed cheerfully. All was quiet. Over on the main road an occasional wheelman, or a few golfers driving to the links, were the only souls that shared with me the freshness of the morning.

Magnolia

A TURN to the right into Summer Street again, and once more to the right into level Raymond Street, brings one between willows and meadows to Magnolia Beach, at the head of Kettle Cove. Here the first comers landed, it is said, and settled Jeffry's Creek, rechristened Manchester, in 1645. The Gloucester line is at the farther end of the beach. The name Magnolia celebrates the beautiful flowers found in the swamps and deep woods which lie to the north.

"Where the Arctic birch is braided by the tropic's
    flowery vines,
  And the white magnolia blossoms star the twilight
    of the pines!"

The beach is edged, after the American manner, with disorderly rows of bathhouses. The settlement beyond, with its cupolas and turrets, seems like a seaside Midway.   To it in summer come seekers for rest and pleasure.   No sharers they of the original settlers'

An Introduction.

prejudices against " excesse in apparrell," " new strainge fashions," nor " superstitious ribbons."   It would be an interesting meeting could Father Time present the maid of that time to the modern woman.

Where the road climbs into the village, and Hunt had his odd studio, " The Hulk,"

Beach at Magnolia.

a stable has been built. Indeed, Magnolia
has greatly changed, and in little more than
a decade. However, many picturesque old

Under the willows, Magnolia.

bits still remain; the old road around the
point under the willows, and by the quaint
fish-houses, is as delightful as ever.

Nowhere does our road come nearer to
the enduring rocks and the clamorous sea
than here. Even on a calm day, the car is

Summer House, Magnolia.

filled with watery noise; the tide is ever
lifting and falling with murmurous cry.

Just above the surf, the path turns away
to pass some fine houses and then follows

a rocky curve, beyond which are the cliffs
by Rafe's Chasm.

In summer this white bulwark of tumbled
rocks, bleaching under the sun, is overhung
by wide, deep masses of sweetbrier, descendants of those same " sweet single roses " that
cheered the Rev. Francis Higginson that
June day in 1629, when the first English
ship sailed adventurously amid the reefs
and ledges along this " Land of Rocks and
Roses." On the tenth of October, I found
one of these same sweet single roses bloom-
ing amid the myriad-gleaming scarlet hips,
and the bunches of asters and faded goldenrod.

At the foot of the decline, a brawling brook
crosses the road, to sink its clamor in the
fuller cadence of the sea.

The road turns from the shore and enters
the wood. Through the trees comes the
music of that little stream : —

> " The music of a brook that flows
> Murmuring farewell, and yet doth never leave."

Over the hill, which is steep, and down the other side about a quarter of a mile, is a little clearing, just where the road stretches away to a level, and here to the right is the path to Rafe's Chasm.

As I walked this path, that October day, the sun shot its warmth through the boughs of the pitch-pines and set free their balsamic odor. Chickadees were calling, and other little birds hopped and flitted about in the branches, too busy to notice me, though I stood within a yard of their work-ground. Bluejays were screaming, and from the distance came the cawing of crows. The boughs rustled a little in the tender breeze, and the birds fluttered gently. Suddenly came the soft, low intermittent pealing of a bell:

> " O father! I hear the church bells ring;
>   Oh say, what may it be ? "

Muffled at times, and not quite like a church-bell, it was the bell-buoy off the Reef of Norman's Woe. Beyond the grove the

"*And the skipper had taken his little daughter,
To bear him company.*"

path is very rough, bordered with bayberry
and ivy, and winds among the sharp spurs
and grass-tufted chinks of the rocks, directly
to Rafe's Chasm.

Here the rock is stripped bare, and rises
bleached gray white on one side but ruddy
on the other. An iron cross set here in the
cliff is in memory of Martha Marion, a
young lady who was swept away by a roller
and drowned.

In the deep chasm, the restless sea roars
and gurgles, or booms hollowly, cadenced by
the sharp swash of the spray. The surf answers the dismal wail of the whistling buoy
at the harbor's mouth. Indeed, the place is
"full of noises," like Prospero's Isle. Across
the bay is Eastern Point and its Light; to
the left, Norman's Woe, peacefully fringed
with white; and beyond, stretching along
the harbor, the roofs and steeples of Gloucester, behind the white sails of its fleet.

When one returns to the road and goes
on toward Gloucester, the sea seems far

away; but any one of the right-hand paths
soon brings it to view. It is all coast or
climb along the shady road, under the wind-
music in the tree-tops. Norman Road, the
way is called at the Magnolia end, and Hes-

Fresh Water Cove Village.

perus Avenue, where it joins the main road
at Fresh Water Village. Fresh Water Cove
lies at the foot of the hill where the fresh
water itself tumbles down the little cascade
under the road. Farther on, the shade falls

Rafe's Chasm.

from unusually fine trees. The road is high
above the bay, and over the water the sunlit
city is framed in the dark embroidery of
the oaks. The road now descends until it
crosses the canal that connects Squam River
with the harbor opposite Ten Pound Island
Light. It wholly loses its charm, and, a little
over three miles from Magnolia, loses itself
in the heart of Gloucester.

Gloucester and Rockport

TILL within a little more than fifty years, Gloucester comprised the whole of Cape Ann. Then the farthermost region was set apart and called Rockport. Gloucester has always reaped her harvest from the sea, and is to-day the foremost fishing-port of the world; while Rockport, though it still sends a fleet to the Banks, rends a part of her living from the granite hills of the Cape itself. But the quarries are a comparatively modern resource. Fishing was the first, and is still the chief,

industry of the people of Cape Ann.   Indeed,
the fisheries brought the first settlers to
our rocky coast, for the sterile Cape itself
offered few attractions.   Behind its rocky
girdle a wild forest rose over tumbled bowlders and ragged ledges.   Only the slender
brooks that trickled down to the shore pierced
its dark mystery; a fearful region it was,
filled, according to the early comers, with
witches and ghosts, lions and devils.   However, the crooked, barren headlands sheltered
snug harbors, and were good places for curing
fish, so along their shores rude fishing villages
were built, — the humble beginnings of to-
day's prosperity.

Active and busy are the streets that have
replaced the rough paths of earlier days.
Banks, churches, offices, and stores line their
length; but even to their most urban parts
comes the cool refreshing breath of the sea.
One is continually reminded of the town's
chief occupation, for the signs read of ships
and their stores, of boats and seines, of nets

From the wharves, East Gloucester.

and fish, and up the side-streets, from the
yards and wharves, steal fine marine odors.
Washington and Main streets lead to East

Main, the road to East Gloucester, with a
most picturesque waterside.   From the store-
houses and fish-flakes, the wharves stretch out
high above the low water, as if on stilts, or are
lapped deeply in the ample flood-tide.   The
fleet crowds the harbor ; and through the maze
of shrouds and masts are seen the towers and
steeples of the city.   On the steep bank that
shelves to the haven, under willows and apple-
trees, cluster snug cottages, and about them
lie boats updrawn in the grasses and flowers.
From the sidepath, one looks down through
green boughs on schooners' decks, on drying seines and dangling purse-nets.

After passing Rocky Neck Avenue, there
is a fine view of the harbor and the surf
breaking at its mouth on Norman's Woe and
the cliffs by Rafe's Chasm.   Here one enters
the land of rackets and golf clubs, summer
girls, novels, and hammocks, water-color kits
and white umbrellas.   Beyond the stone gate-
house, the way swings around the sunny curve
of a sandy beach, then through the shade of

rustling poplars and great willows, close by Niles Pond. Over its fresh water, the ocean stretches, a deeper blue; and the noise of the far off surf forms an undertone to the

Eastern Point.

song of birds and the splashing of the pond's thin waves on the mossy rocks. All the way to Eastern Point, the fields are bossed with rocks, and gay with flowers. From the shrub-

The Harbor from East Gloucester.

bery, comes the continual song of birds.   The
farther one goes, the louder becomes the un-
ceasing refrain of the surf, the clearer the intermittent peal of the floating bell, the stronger
the melancholy wail of the whistling buoy.

Beyond the rusty wall of jumbled rocks, by
the light-house on Eastern Point, the outgoing
fleet, meeting the broad Atlantic swell, tosses
and tips like the little ships on old Dutch
clocks.   The afternoon sun blazes on the
harbor; the sails of the tacking schooners
alternate in sunlight or shadow ; and the hills
at Magnolia gleam softly green, or sink darkly
purple, into the fleeting cloud-shadows.   Bayberry and wild roses perfume the sea-air.

My last visit here was preceded by a long
spell of foul weather ; and so, with the promise
of fair winds and blue skies, many vessels
were beating out of the harbor, and passing
in quick procession about the Point.   The
offing was all flecked with their sails.   " Cap-
tains Courageous," and crews as brave, were
putting forth to their perilous toil among

the fogs and tempests of the Banks, whence many a ship has returned with flag half-masted, for few callings are so dangerous. Hundreds of Gloucester widows and orphans mourn their lost ones, perished in those treacherous seas.

It may be that the dangers, the sufferings, and the calamities of a fisherman's life in this world inspired the sweet doctrine of an all-forgiving Mercy in the hereafter which found such a ready acceptance on the Cape, for the Universalist sect was established here as early as 1770, and John Murray, its apostle, preached for many years in the old Universalist church at Gloucester.

Certainly, the adventurous life of the fishermen was well calculated to fit them for daring naval deeds; and so we find that, during the Revolution and the War of 1812, the sailors of Gloucester were a scourge to the British. Captain Haraden alone wrested 1000 cannon from them on the high seas. The hardy industry of this people is the school of heroes.

From the light-house at Eastern Point, the road winds close to the shore, and in the distance there soon glimmer the buttresses of Brace's Rock.   It seems to me that this should be the very spot where John Josselyn, Gent., in 1638, saw his monster, the sea-serpent, "quoiled up on a rock at Cape Ann." I can imagine his shaggy head reposing on the great green-backed rock that first shoulders off the surges, and his crimson mottled " quoils " luxuriously cooled by the dazzling bouquets of foam that break on the purple and sienna ramparts of his lair.

Close by the path, at the head of Brace's Cove, Niles Pond again appears, sparkling amid its lily pads and sedge, so that you have on one side, the expanse of the ocean, breaking rollers, passing ships, and wheeling gulls, and on the other side, dimpling fresh water, under the shade of willows, water-lily blossoms, swaying-reeds and sweet-voiced landbirds.   Farther on, from a hill, a grand view of the harbor is spread out, and the road

leads us back to the city. For the shore
cannot be followed conveniently all around the
Cape. I pushed my wheel through its rocky
pastures, and over its beaches, which last is
possible at low water ; but the better way is
to start afresh from the city, Whittier's "Cool
and sea-blown town."

The long country road across the Cape
is known as Eastern Avenue in Gloucester,
but becomes Main Street in Rockport. The
electric cars now tear noisily, and at breakneck
speed, through the lonely woods it traverses.
To this day, the interior of the Cape is about
as wild and untamed as ever. It was doubt-
less in the shades and silence of this forest
that the ghostly host was bred which
descended in 1692 on the garrison of Cape
Ann ; for a part in the troublous witchcraft
times was not denied to Gloucester, though
it was happily neither sad nor cruel.

It was, we are told, in the summer of the
year so fateful to Salem, that "rollicking
apparitions dressed, like gentlemen, in white
waistcoats and breeches," kept the good

Ebenezer Babson.

people here " in feverish excitement and
alarm, for a whole fortnight together." At
first, only a couple of these " rollicking
apparitions" were discovered by one Ebenezer
Babson, a sturdy yeoman of Cape Ann;
but their number soon increased, keeping
pace with the number of the witnesses of
their evil pranks. These jovial demons
disported themselves in a manner quite
rowdyish and more becoming to gentlemen
of the eighteenth century and the mother
country, than to staid Puritan times and prim
New England. They skulked about in the
bushes, threw stones, beat on barns with
clubs, were insolent in some outlandish jargon
(probably hog-Latin!), and even made one
or two bad shots at the sturdy yeoman.
Indeed, " they acted more in the spirit of
diabolical revelry, than as if actuated by any
deadlier purpose; " and this farce they kept
up, though much powder and ball were
wasted on them by Babson and his comrades,
who were actually reinforced by a detachment
of sixty men from Ipswich, led by Captain

Appleton! According to the poet Whittier, the discerning Captain, after firing a silver button at the merry gentlemen with no effect, declared them to be no mortal foes, turned to his Bible, and then lifted up his voice in prayer, amid his kneeling men.

" Ceased thereat the mystic marching of the spectres round the wall,
  But a sound abhorred, unearthly, smote the ears and hearts of all, —
  Howls of rage and shrieks of anguish ! Never after, mortal man
  Saw the ghostly leaguers marching round the block-house of Cape Ann."

Later on, Gloucester had a resident witch also, one Margaret Wesson, who was long the dread of the superstitious dwellers on the Cape. But, in 1745, they were delivered of her in a strange and mysterious manner. At the siege of Louisburg by the Colonial troops, two Massachusetts soldiers, natives of Gloucester, were annoyed by the persistent and unusual actions of an uncanny crow that hovered over them, cawing horribly.

"*Old Meg.*"

.

One of them thought that under this black disguise he recognized " Old Meg," as Gloucester's witch was called. So he and his comrade cut each a silver button off his uniform, and fired them at the crow. " At the first shot, they broke its leg ; at the second, it fell dead at their feet." Thus are we at once impressed by the excellence of their marksmanship, and the munificence of the Colonial government in the matter of buttons. However, the strangest part of the story follows. Home again, our two soldiers learned that on the precise day, hour, and minute when they had killed the suspicious crow, Old Meg herself had unaccountably fallen of a broken leg, and soon after died in great agony. And, stranger still, upon examining her wounds, the identical silver buttons were found with which the soldiers had loaded their guns under the walls of Louisburg. And this story, as well as the one of the Spectre Leaguers, was " vouched for by persons of character and credibility."

After coming out of the woods, there is
a wide-reaching view of the ocean over the
tree-tops and rocky pastures ; then Main Street

The Main Street, Rockport.

dips quickly toward Sandy Bay. The way
to Land's End is around to the right and
close to the water. It is a pleasant street
that winds by old houses and wayside wells

Rockport.

through the heart of the town, by the village church, to the little common under its elms. Next, comes Mt. Pleasant Street, and a good climb past more old houses with square massive chimneys, and gardens bright with old-fashioned flowers. Through their orchards and over their sloping fields is seen the deep blue of the sea.

But the way soon becomes a country road; over its length rise the towers of the lights on Thatcher's Island. The road is at a considerable distance from the water, and the fields slope down to Loblolly Cove. A little back, on the left, are Straitsmouth Island and light, and the Tri-Salvages reef and spindle, tapering out to sea.

Thatcher's Island was first named Thatcher's Woe by Anthony Thatcher, to commemorate the sad story of his shipwreck there in August, 1635. His own family of seven, that of his cousin Parson Avery, numbering eleven, and five others — in all, twenty-three souls — set sail from Ipswich, for Marblehead, to whose rough fisher-folk the Rev. Mr. Avery felt called to preach the Gospel. All went well until the night of August fourteenth, when, at ten o'clock, their old sails split. They then resolved to cast anchor till morning ; but, before daylight, a mighty storm arose, and, their cable slipping away, the pinnace was hurled by the raging seas upon a rock. Nearly the whole ship's company were swallowed up, or dashed to pieces by the merciless waves. Thatcher and his wife were both saved, as if by a miracle. He called the desolate island upon which they were cast away Thatcher's Woe, after his own name, "and the Rock, Avery, his Fall, to the end that their fall and loss, and mine own, might be had in perpetual remembrance." In the isle lieth buried the body of his cousin's eldest daughter, whom he found dead on the shore. Whittier's poem, "The Swan Song of Parson Avery," is founded on this history.

" And still the fishers outbound, or scudding from the
        squall,
    With grave and reverent faces, the ancient tale recall,
    When they see the white waves breaking on the
        Rock of Avery's Fall ! "

The road continues to the Turk's Head Inn, at Land's End, which is named for its proto-type in Cornwall. On the beach here, just back from Milk Island, the Atlantic cable is brought up out of the sea, and is marked by two curiously striped poles with discs. Here the road ends. Beyond, stretches the length of Long Beach to Bass Rocks.

Thatcher's, Straitsmouth, and Milk Islands were called, by Capt. John Smith, the Three Turks' Heads, in memory of one of his exploits, when, as a Christian champion, he slew as many Turks in combat and afterwards beheaded them. To this grisly souvenir, he added a pleasanter one, by naming Cape Ann, Cape Tragabizanda, after a fair Moslem who beguiled the weary days of his captivity in Stamboul.

> "Who, when the chance of war had bound
> The Moslem chain his limbs around,
> Soothed with her smiles his hours of pain,
> And fondly to her youthful slave
> A dearer gift than freedom gave."

IF in Rockport, at the foot of the hill from
Gloucester, one turns to the left, instead of
towards Land's End, the road will take him
about Sandy Bay, and then above the artificial
harbors to which the granite is brought from
the quarries of Pole and Pigeon Hills. In its
descent, the rocky debris has crept outward
till it lies like a petrified octopus, with rigid
arms stretched out into the sea. One cannot
help wondering how the beauty of ledge and
bowlder can be transformed into such ugliness.
The air is filled with the tinkle of hammer
and chisel, and the testy puff of steam-drills.
Occasionally, comes the boom of an explo-
sion, wresting the rocks from the hills.

From the road itself, one may look down
into a quarry, with its tracks and engines,

its sheds and steam-drills, and its men, ant-like, beneath the high derricks.   The wayside houses are utilitarian and unlovely, yet sometimes not without a lowly picturesqueness.

It is uphill and down between the blue wall of the sea and the gray granite hills, to Pigeon Cove at the harbor, and then up the hill on the other side, with houses of a better class, and many summer hotels and boarding houses.

At the top of the hill, a drive leads seaward along the shore by Andrew's Point and Hoop Pole Cove, and back to Granite Street.   The summer settlement here is called Ocean View. The rocky shore is well-wooded, exposed to the full fury of the northeasters; and the surf is often magnificent.

Granite Street runs into Washington Street, and over its sloping length, across the wind-whipped bay, shine the sands of Plum Island, glimmering in their own heat, and backed by the hills of Newbury.   At the foot of the slope is Folly Cove, lonely and grim, and across it Folly Point, its strata defined

by sombre markings, now sloping, now
vertical, to the white foam at its foot. A
few fisher-huts are
clustered at the head
of the cove, dories are
drawn far above the
reach of waves, and

Folly Cove

the fences are festooned with drying nets, in
all the shades of brown and black. From
here, the road climbs a little hill beside a

" The Village Street."

brook tumbling down its granite bed. Where
the roads fork, the perspective of lower lane
is spaced by level shadows from bordering
willows, their trunks cut darkly across the
green meadow.   Beyond is Lanesville.

The prettier way, by Langsford Street, runs
uphill by an oak grove and under old locusts.
Soon the sea comes in sight, and on its rim,
over the open fields, Agamenticus in Maine
rises blue and alone.   Then the coast shows
faintly off Portsmouth, and by Rye and Hamp-
ton to Salisbury Beach, where the cottages
loom white on the sands; and over the end of
the road is the purple of Heartbreak Hill in
Ipswich.

As I stood here, a stone schooner was
standing out from Bay View in the fresh north-
west wind.   So heavily was she laden, that
her deck was scarcely above water.   She did
not seem to list at all under the strong breeze,
though all sail was set.   So deep was she,
that as the seas struck her, they swept back
across her deck from stem to stern.   The

afternoon sun lit up her sails and cast a long
shadow over the water in her lee.

Great heaps of paving-stones for the armor-
ing of city streets lie piled by the harbor.
Along the shaded village street of Lanesville,
the houses cluster, and between them and
the sea are great sloping granite promontories, in their hollows fertile green-sward and
thriving, though wind-tossed, willows.   When
a northeast gale sweeps this coast, the tormented sea, ridged and edged by foam, rushes
wildly along Folly Point, breaking in white
fury against the rocks all the way to
Lane's Cove, then hurries on till spent in
smothered foam over the tusks of Plum
Cove Ledge.

At Bay View, a deep inlet makes in almost
to the road; beyond the village, on a hill, is
the First Universalist church of Annisquam.
Square and box-like it stands, under a spread-
ing elm, overlooking Lobster Cove.   The
afternoon sun glitters on the shore and water
of this deep cut in the granite hills.   Fruit-
trees, overtopped by whispering pines, bend

Annisquam Church.

over its edge, vines and grasses straggle down
its tumbling walls.

A square old-fashioned house, with great
central chimney, stands at the beginning of
the winding country road to Annisquam.
This is a quiet little haven, resting under its
fruit and shade trees, sheltered by granite hills
that rise steeply between it and the sea, on
one side, and the bowlder-strewn Cape hills
on the other. No matter how the wind may
blow outside, the little cove is placid. The
houses are mostly snug cottages, many of
them very picturesque. Here and there, is a
mouldering boat by a decrepit wharf, or a dory
drawn up or afloat, or an old-fashioned well,
— in fact the place abounds in artistic bits
of foreground. All about Cape Ann, one will
notice how common and how various are the
wayside wells. Past the post-office and
school, the road turns at the head of the harbor to the west side of the hill, where there is
a summer settlement by Cambridge people.
It is at the head of Squam River, across which
are the fantastic shifting dunes of Coffin's

beach and the sands of Castle Neck in
Ipswich.

Head of Annisquam Harbor.

From the main street near the post-office,
the way to Gloucester is over the old wooden
bridge, over which the stage-coach has ceased

to clatter. It was a noisy crossing, made not without apprehension. Even under a passing wheel, the old draw creaks complainingly.

At the head of the cove, the little church shines white above the green ring of trees, and, in leafy shadows, a schooner or two seem like interlopers in this land-locked quiet.

Across the bridge we come again to Washington Street, then another bridge, and so, under a long aisle of arching willows, to Riverdale. The picturesque quality of the way here is leaving it fast; it is not as pleasant a ride or walk as it used to be.

Close by the tide-mill is the monument to the " Riverdale Martyrs," under the shadow of the flag. Above the dam, the calm waters reflect steep-faced Beacon Pole Hill, and below, the water tumbles noisily into an arm of Squam River, stretching out attractively between Riverdale and Wheeler's Point.

The road rises to the foot of Beacon Pole Hill. From this elevation, I looked across the green fertile meadows and calm stream. The

rough hills, with a virile, bossy decoration of
thickly strewn bowlders, caught on their
shoulders the golden evening light. The

Riverdale.

shadow, creeping upward with purple edge,
melted into rich olive in the hollow, from the
mingling of lichen-colored rocks and thin,

cropped turf. Beyond, in the south, over the roofs of Gloucester, in the last ray of sunset, glistened the golden cross of Saint Anne's.

It is now only a short wheel back to Gloucester. There finishes the bicycle path along the Puritan Coast, and here this book comes also to its End.

THE END

www.ingramcontent.com/pod-product-compliance
Lightning Source LLC
Chambersburg PA
CBHW030323270326
41926CB00010B/1483